MIRACLES AND MILESTONES

THE INCREDIBLE ODYSSEY OF
A FIRE DISPATCHER FROM OHIO,
TO 9/11, AND BEYOND

Book Design & Production:
Columbus Publishing Lab
www.ColumbusPublishingLab.com

Copyright © 2025 by
Christopher Carver

All rights reserved.
This book, or parts thereof, may not be
reproduced in any form without permission.

Paperback ISBN: 978-1-63337-994-7
E-Book ISBN: 978-1-63337-995-4

Printed in the United States of America
1 3 5 7 9 10 8 6 4 2

MIRACLES AND MILESTONES

THE INCREDIBLE ODYSSEY OF A FIRE DISPATCHER FROM OHIO, TO 9/11, AND BEYOND

CHRISTOPHER BLAKE CARVER

*"The safest road to Hell is the gradual one—
the gentle slope, soft underfoot, without sudden turnings,
without milestones, without signposts."*

—C.S. Lewis, The Screwtape Letters

CONTENTS

Foreword		i
Introduction		iii
Chapter 1:	September 2016	1
Chapter 2:	The Blackout of August 2003	13
Chapter 3:	The Early Years	27
Chapter 4:	Awakenings	35
Chapter 5:	Avoidance	41
Chapter 6:	The Fire Department Journey Begins	51
Chapter 7:	Coming Out	59
Chapter 8:	Miracle on Town Street	63
Chapter 9:	The Test	67
Chapter 10:	The Plan	73
Chapter 11:	Survival	77
Chapter 12:	Getting Settled in NYC	89
Chapter 13:	Foundations and Beginnings	97
Chapter 14:	Training and Onboarding	103
Chapter 15:	Summer of 2001	115
Chapter 16:	September 10, 2001	127
Chapter 17:	September 11, 2001, about 10:00 a.m.	135
Chapter 18:	The Brooklyn Central Office on September 11, 2001	145
Chapter 19:	The After	155
Chapter 20:	September 12 and Beyond	157
Chapter 21:	Returning to Normalcy?	165
Chapter 22:	March 11, 2002	169
Chapter 23:	June 2002	173
Chapter 24:	September 11, 2002	179
Chapter 25:	Deutsche Bank, August 2007	183
Chapter 26:	Superstorm Sandy	189
Chapter 27:	For what purpose?	197
Afterword		209
Photos		215
Acknowledgements		221
About the Author		225

FOREWORD

Readers should be aware that this book does not fit into established non-fiction categories. Although unconventional in the breadth of topics, this work reflects insights and experiences gathered along my unorthodox journey. An odyssey that took me from adopted kid in Ohio, to out gay person, to being a part of an incredible group of FDNY professionals with whom I served for a variety of major emergencies including Blackouts, Blizzards, fires and September 11th, 2001.

Perhaps separate books could have addressed each of the principal areas of focus. But that was not the way I lived my life and that certainly was not the way my life lived me. The major moments shared here all led to others, increasing their impact in unexpected ways. As I look back at those events and experiences with something approaching a small degree of wisdom, I can see a tapestry impossible to appreciate as the events actually unfolded. Our many discarded and unrealized life plans, goals, and other arrogant attempts at control and certainty reveal that God often looks at our planners or calendars, chuckles a bit, and does exactly what **God** wants to do. In my case, what God did can only be described as miraculous. Complicated, painful, and sometimes terrifying, but a journey that led me to where I now claim a sense of purpose, place and connection. I now understand how transformative those unexplainable, yet interdependent events were and can be, not just for individuals, but also for organizations and communities.

That does not justify the horrible things that happen. The greeting card platitude that all things happen for a reason is painfully trite and simplistic. How do we ever justify the unjustifiable? But we do have to move forward from the unimagined and unexpected days of horror to someplace different. If we forever remain in that darkness, then the horrible event completes its conquest, and we remain forever its victim.

There is another option. The unexpected and unplanned can offer us the glimpse of a forward path. A distant point from which we can look back with understanding, maybe even granting ourselves a self-appreciating "pat on the back" that we did not collapse permanently under grief, anger or fear. Some of the worst of our disappointments may even open cracks that not only allow the "light in," to paraphrase Leonard Cohen, but create space for understanding and grace, both for ourselves and others. That was the miracle on the other side of some of my worst days. Hopefully, sharing my story of darkness and light will help others to at least imagine a place on the other side of their own worst days.

INTRODUCTION

It's often a simple question, asked to the point of annoyance by a child to their parent. Why can't I lick the glue stick? Why can't I pull the dog's tail or consume every single cookie in the box in one sitting? We get older, and sometimes wiser, but never fully escape the question "why?" Instead, it becomes much more "adult." Why did our parents do the things they did? Why did a beloved friend make a questionable life choice? Why does the world seem so out of control?

In our presumed maturity, "why?" even evolves from a question into a silent pleading prayer: a brave but often futile attempt to understand the motives of the Creator in the face of the unexplainable.

I am no exception.

September 11th, 2001, is the principal day of "why" in my professional and personal life. On that day, I had the profound honor of being a part of the New York City Fire Department (FDNY), as a fire alarm dispatcher. By September of 2001, I had been living in New York City for a little over a year, just one of the countless people who find their way to the Gotham madness in search of…something. It was also a Tuesday and—my twenty-seventh birthday.

I stood there, a little after 10:00 a.m., looking up at what felt like all the evil ever known in the world distilled into one raging black cloud swirling over my home, my community, my friends. All the world cast into shadow in an attempt to sew hate, division and fear.

They wanted to generate fear in as many people as possible, not just in New York but around the United States and across the globe. In that, they did succeed. With just a little space or quiet, I can still access that fear today. The emotion lives just under the surface, in the same internal neighborhood as the biggest doubts and questions I have always wondered about in my life. All of that came rolling forward on September 11th, 2001, and in the days and years after.

Why had I ended up there, at that moment, and in that place? How and why were the dispatchers of FDNY able to manage September 11, 2001, and its aftermath despite its scale and scope exceeding anything ever faced by a fire department? Why was this a part of the plan of my life? How would it be possible to move forward?

In the days and weeks that followed, there were more questions, especially as September 11th 2001 evolved to just "9/11" and the incident itself transitioned from an emergency to a national holiday, and our task changed from managing a response to coordinating a commemoration. Why is it so important to recognize that day? Is it a holiday just because of the horror and the loss and scars, or are there more profound insights and lessons to be gathered from our generation's Pearl Harbor?

In a review of my experiences before, during, and after September 11th at least some answers to those questions are revealed. It was on that day that I was able to live into the power of community as people rallied with and held those who were lost, those who were saved, and those who did the saving. I was able to see firsthand the power of connection between citizen strangers and the danger of what can happen when people forsake their humanity. I was able to experience, up close, first from the street in my neighborhood and then on the other end of radio transmissions, phone calls and complex recovery operations, the power of a team committed to the purpose of saving lives no matter the complexity of the challenge or the human cost of that effort. I was able to experience the aftermath and work through the recovery, of an organization, and a city, on the circuitous path back to something like normalcy. I was able to witness, even in the face of a tragedy beyond my imagination, the miraculous—as people from varied walks of life and an infinite number of backgrounds helped their fellow citizens make it through that day and what followed.

Certainly, the event was the farthest thing from a miracle, but in the response and in the recovery was found something so far beyond the expectations of human behavior that it qualifies as countless miracles, great and small. Likewise, those miracles can be found in the path of unique, wonderous, and terrifying experiences that brought me to intersect with that day and what happened after.

The questions and answers surrounding September 11th, 2001 have become more important with time, distance, and space. Both my personal experiences and those of the organization and communities I was a part of offer lessons even more valuable today than immediately after. As history fades from firsthand recollection into scrapbooks, historical collections, and archives, there is a risk that 9/11 will descend into what might best be called glorified propaganda. It could become a flag waving tribute with singing chorus but too little serious reflection or remembrance. With that evolution, it is a tragic possibility that some of the real lessons of 9/11 will be lost or ignored.

We might forget that it takes a valued, trusted, and empowered group of diverse professionals for any organization or team to succeed. We may think that only some team members can contribute in the face of a complex and demanding emergency. Individuals may assume they will never have to rise above a minimum level of effort or competence. Or that will never have to bravely take the initiative without someone else telling them exactly what to do when the normal rules and procedures are long past relevant. In our crazy bitter time we may focus only on the worst of human nature and live lives encased in fear, bitterness, and resolute certainty. These are just some of the things we must resist if September

11th is going to be more than just a day of flags, tears, remembrance, and disconnected history.

For those who work in public safety and emergency services, there is another risk. We may lose our understanding of and appreciation for the personal and professional systems, actions, and decisions that allowed 9/11 to be managed in the face of all its complexity and terror. We may believe that technology alone can solve our human challenges and mitigate complex incidents.

The events and experiences shared in this book may help us avoid those outcomes. My journey has revealed in many different ways how we can make it through our own September 11ths and all the other incredibly difficult days we face—beginning and ending with community and connection, whether as an individual or organization.

Whether in our neighborhood, our firehouse, or our 9-1-1 Center, it will always be the courageous and dedicated people that help us to succeed, to find a way forward, and show us a way through the black who offer the greatest inspiration and most important reminders. Sometimes that courageous person is found in others, sometimes looking back in our own mirror—but most often it is found in the planned and unplanned moments and people with whom we share the mysterious, wonderous, tragic and glorious adventure that is our life. Finding, even when it seems all hope is lost, some way forward.

1 SEPTEMBER 2016

The two days were hauntingly similar but five hundred miles and over a decade apart. Skies were indescribably bright, sun-filled, deep blue to almost black in color, no clouds to be seen. Temperatures were pleasant, especially for the wildly variable time just after Labor Day. Both days had that just-past-summer, fall-closing-in feeling of potential, excitement, and change.

Although the skies and feelings were similar, they might as well have taken place on different planets. They reflected two different worlds. One found in 2001, the other in 2016. In 2016, in a midsize suburban Ohio community, a group of residents and community officials gathered to commemorate a terrorist attack. In 2001, at about the same time on the same date in September, five hundred miles away in New York City, an equally diverse group of people trudged off to work in office towers, firehouses, schools, and shops. In 2001, the residents of New York were completely unaware that they were walking into one of those days of history that was a momentous turning point. There would be a distinct before and after. By the time the sun set on September 11, 2001, things would never be the same.

What happened on that September morning in 2001 would lead directly to the event I was part of in 2016 in Westerville, Ohio as well as thousands of other events like it in towns and cities across America and the world. These ceremonies would commemorate the before and the after. They would help people remember just what happened on a pristine late-summer morning in New York City, Arlington, Virginia, Shanksville, Pennsylvania, and the hearts and minds of everyone alive to experience the day known as 9/11.

On September 11, 2016, as part of that effort to remember and remind, I was delivering a speech at a 9/11 commemoration event. I was also desperately trying to overcome a brisk wind that made keeping the paper copy of my speech in place nearly impossible.

I tried to use a pen and then a nearby rock to hold the pages down, but they were determined to take flight. I wondered to myself what would happen if my prepared remarks suddenly landed in the middle of the nearby street. Did I know enough of what I would say to wing it? Would anyone notice if I did? I finally found a way to tilt myself at just the right angle to create a block from the wind and some degree of protection for the several hundred words I would be sharing with the assembled crowd. Still, that did little to calm my nerves. I began.

> "Good afternoon and thank you all for attending. I would like to take a moment and acknowledge the Reverend David C. Hogg and Westerville Fire Chief Brian Miller for inviting me to share just a little about my 9/11 experience and the efforts of my fellow FDNY fire dispatchers, supervisors, and New Yorkers.
>
> "My name is Christopher Blake Carver. I am a proud Reynoldsburg and Ohio State grad who managed to make happen a dream of living in the "big city" and of working for the nation's greatest fire department. That dream brought me into the path of the event we are here to remember today—a day that also happens to be my birthday.
>
> "It is my honor to share my story—*our* story—but it is my *hope* that you will take at least a little of this message home

and not leave it among the flags and the steel and the tears that are so often part of these events.

"I have heard it asked why, fifteen years on, are these 9/11 ceremonies so important? Why should we take time out to reflect on *where we were* and *who* we were on that beautiful Tuesday morning that suddenly changed our nation and us forever? What does that time teach us?

"Perhaps the first reason why ceremonies like this are so important can be found in a number: fifty-nine million. That is the number of babies born just in this country since September 11, 2001. For them, they will always know 9/11 as a story, as a history lesson, with answers on some test that they will take or have taken in a class they maybe won't appreciate. It is an event almost as distant to them as the Founding Fathers are to us, or the sinking of the *Maine* or, increasingly, World War Two. Important, yes, but not connected, not *real*.

"For the rest of us, who know where we were, what we were doing, how it felt to watch those images, we need no reminder that was so very real. We require no CliffsNotes.

"In fact, for many people, it is more than a memory even today. It is something that they live with each day, some better than others, some worse. At best, it is something just under the surface.

"Just last night, shortly before midnight, I found myself consoling a friend about that day. Even though his father survived being in the towers that morning, the fear and the terror still live front and center in his mind. I know he is not alone."

I could not help but think of another September 11 while sharing my words. It was September 11, 2002 when I last felt that same type of nervousness as on that day in Ohio. It was a similar task, although the audience was mainly on the other end of a microphone, and I was safely indoors. It was also not a solo engagement. As part of a team of fire dispatchers, I was reading a speech that had been fully scripted with zero room for creativity or adjusting on the fly. I was one of three New York City fire alarm dispatchers in the Bronx Communications Office tasked with performing one of the FDNYs most solemn traditions—announcing the "four fives" to the firehouses and firefighters of the Bronx on the first anniversary of the September 11 attacks. The "four fives" were a connection back to the days when the department communicated by telegraph. They sent the signal of four number fives in a row over the bell system to order every FDNY firehouse to lower flags to half-staff, most often in honor of a firefighter who had been lost in the line of duty. Over the years, the process had evolved to consist of a voice announcement, which followed a very disciplined script that was read over the department's intercom system and radio frequencies, along with a typed message to the department's teleprinter system. In 2002, each of the five boroughs still had its fire central or communications office that served as the home of the Fire Dispatchers responsible for a section of New York City.

In all five offices, on that September 2002 morning, dispatchers prepared to do something that had never been done. We would announce three-hundred-forty-three line of duty deaths in one comprehensive roll. The most significant number of firefighters previously lost in one event had been twelve killed in the infamous 23rd Street fire and collapse of October 17, 1966, close to where the Flatiron Building still stands near Madison Square Park in Manhattan.

Although the number we would announce that morning was almost incomprehensible, the format and cadence were the same as always. The FDNY dispatchers tasked with reading performed a nearly religious role and a critical element of the grieving process for our department and city. The scale of the events of September 11, 2001, and the losses of the FDNY on that day, meant what had been the routine timing procedures of *when to* announce were not possible. The department had tried. In the first weeks, we announced the "four fives" as soon as possible after the remains of members were identified and their families notified. However, it had become apparent early on, in the shadows of the still-smoking remains of the towers, that recovery and even identification would be far more complex and time-consuming than anyone could imagine.

In response, the department decided to announce every September 11, 2001 related line of duty death in one massive process of procedure, mourning, and grief. It would be a singular September 11, 2001, roll call of those who would never return home to their firehouses or homes and who, in the performance of their duty, effected the most incredible rescue of civilians from a fire in American history. The announcement was straightforward. The details were few but precise. Race, religion, nationality, sexual orientation, time on the job, favorite football team, or any other supplemental personal characteristics were omitted. It was title, rank, and company, accompanied by the summary "as a result of injuries sustained while operating at Manhattan Fifth Alarm Box 8087, transmitted at 08:47 hours on September 11, 2001."

All the ways we have found to distinguish ourselves from community and illustrate differentiation were discarded in favor of an elegant, precise, and traditional declaration about the loss in terms of something far more significant: the role that each lost member played as part of the world's greatest fire department on its greatest and most tragic day. It was far less the words of an obituary than the acknowledgment of the service and sacrifice of individuals who were part of something so much bigger than even they had realized. Their required duties came into focus with the sight of the Twin Towers of the World Trade Center on fire and potentially thousands of people in need of rescue.

When the announcement started at 08:47 on September 11, 2002, the same time as the initial alarm had been transmitted, a fierce wind picked up in New York City. It ended immediately after the last name was read. The process took over an hour, but with the honored duty finally having been completed. In one sense, a chapter was now closed, but in another, something was just beginning. Anytime a firefighter is lost in the line of duty, they become a part of something much bigger. They are not just a name on the wall of FDNY headquarters or a plaque in their firehouses. They are part of a collective understanding and memory of the sacrifice and duty required to help ensure the safety of residents and visitors to America's largest city. This duty has been part of the department's history since the day it was founded in 1865. This reading and announcement were integral but in no way the initial or final chapter.

My task on that September morning in Ohio in 2016 was, in some ways, like the reading of the "four fives." I shared the collective story of what September 11, 2001 had meant to our department and our city, and what it should mean to those who were not there and maybe were not even alive at the time.

A high school friend who was serving as Westerville's fire chief had invited me to speak. A collection of local dignitaries was there: mayors, city council people, and other public safety chiefs. Everyone was positioned around a memorial plaza dedicated to those who had given their all on September 11, 2001. There were also several hundred residents. My words took about fifteen minutes. Within them, I tried to share the perspective of someone who went to work on September 11, 2001 in the FDNY, who saw the smoke, who smelled the horror, and who helped in some small way manage the aftermath.

My goal was to tell the people of Westerville, Ohio what they should know about what happened. I assumed no one else in the crowd had been in New York City that day. I also assumed no one there had been a part of the fire department, police department, or any other organization responsible for responding to one of the most challenging emergencies in American history.

Yes, hundreds, perhaps thousands, of people from public safety organizations around the world came to New York City to help in the aftermath, and their contributions were invaluable and appreciated, but their experiences were somewhat different. It was not their homes that smelled of smoke months after. It was not their favorite bookstore buried under 110 floors of debris. It was not their co-workers who were forced to find some way to power through the aftermath of 9/11 collectively. It was primarily not their friends whose names were read out in our solemn rituals of remembrance or their neighbors who were forced to find their way through a type of universal post-traumatic stress disorder.

Geology teaches that earthquakes are much more powerful based on how close you are to the epicenter, not just in their damage to buildings and structures, but also in their impact on our memory and our lives. The same was true with 9/11 for those of us who lived in New York City and worked for the FDNY and other New York City public safety organizations.

Scientists have now established an understanding that trauma can be passed down from one generation to the next, a DNA-coded memory of collective experiences that impact entire groups of people in mysterious and unanticipated ways. If that is true—that an event as horrifying and world-changing as 9/11 can be passed on—then it made my effort that day in Westerville and in the pages of this book even more important. The explanation for that shadow trauma is not necessarily carried along with the sensation. That requires some work to decipher, to help illustrate and help explain so those who come after can have some hope of understanding a scar they were not alive to see or feel created.

On that Ohio morning, struggling to save my speech from flying into traffic, my words focused on the service and the teamwork of the firefighters, EMTs, law enforcement personnel, and dispatchers. I shared how everyone came together to manage the response to an event beyond imagination. I shared how civilians, residents, and other non-responders pulled together to help each other escape Lower Manhattan and make their way home. I shared how those of us in New York were helped by people from all over the world to overcome the sadness and trauma of devastating loss. Collectively, we celebrated the memories of those who were lost and then tried to find a way forward, even in a city covered by the smoke from smoldering fires for weeks after the attention of the world drifted elsewhere. I tried to explain how the largest city in America came together like a small Midwestern town on that day and for months after. I relayed a little about a journey that led me from growing up in suburban Columbus, Ohio to being a part of the world's greatest fire department.

I titled the speech "I Have Seen Miracles." It focused on the heroism, sacrifice, and service that surrounded the events of September 11, 2001. Even in the face of unspeakable horror, you could find the miraculous if you choose to take the time to look for it and recognize it.

However, in the case of my story, it was so much more than miraculous events around that one day and its aftermath. It was an entire collection of people, places, and events which reflected the miraculous potential in our human journey. From people who supported me or helped me, to those who challenged me in good ways, to those who gave me a new life before I was even three days old, the path that led me to 9/11/01 was incredible. It was not all good, however. Events both terrible and wonderful led me to that podium to commemorate the place I had been and what I had borne witness to fifteen years earlier. It had always been about human connection. The great days were made better by connection; the bad days were made bearable in the same way. I described this in that speech in 2016.

> "Shocked back into humanity by the events of 9/11, New Yorkers came to know quickly that we needed each other, that we depended on each other. This is always true in New York City, especially on a neighborhood level. But for those six months, maybe a year, it was at a citywide level. New

York City truly became the biggest small town in America. People spoke to each other on the street, people smiled, people slowed down just a bit. It was pretty crazy, but it was also pretty wonderful. As many of you may know, New York is a very diverse place. People of all faiths, all religions, all histories, living as one. In those days, weeks, and months after 9/11, we were even more of a melting pot, and a beautiful example of just how united these United States can be when we make the time to care for on another. I think of those 8.5 million people, living and healing together, when someone asks what should we remember about 9/11 or what we need to teach about that day to those who did not live through it."

The journey that took me from suburban Ohio and a planned career as an international diplomat to being a fire dispatcher, and ultimately, the director of FDNY fire dispatch, has been full of miracles. However, it was also full of challenges, struggles, frustration, and fear.

The same observation applies to the communities in which we find ourselves today, many years later. We wonder how we can come together to overcome the issues we face in our world, or if it is even possible. However, in doubting the possibility of improvement, we forget in an instant the essential lessons of September 11, 2001, and the other "impossible" hurdles we have managed to overcome as a community. It should come as no shock, but it is still terribly sad, that only a couple of decades after its stunning imprint was left on our collective lives, the lessons of 9/11 appear to have faded. If social media, news, and politicians are to be believed, our world seems on the verge of splintering into permanent camps, like our tribal ancestors. This world is unwilling to accept, much less celebrate, the wondrous possibilities that come from living and working together with others, no matter how different they may be. We should focus on our shared humanity rather than the stressors and grievances modern society too often forces us to embrace. The "algorithms" do not do well with community, connection, and collaboration, and neither do the counts of "clicks."

Along the path of my personal and professional life, I have been fortunate to experience events that have offered near-constant reminders of these hard but essential truths. It has been shown to me over and over that finding the opportunity to connect and overcome starts with understanding our place, purpose, and role. It continues with acknowledging, even for brief moments, what we have the power to do. It also requires us to accept and even celebrate that we cannot and must not do our most challenging work alone. In the smoke and dust of a battered city, so much of the illusion of difference immediately faded away. It is not too dramatic to say we all look the same under the coat of ghostly ash or in the massed crowd desperate for news about missing loved ones, clamoring for comfort in the face of terrible tragedy.

The best organizations, teams, and communities can leverage this connectedness, sometimes without even realizing it. In the story of September 11, 2001, and other memorable dates before and since, some stories and insights can serve as reminders that can benefit everyone. It is not necessary for all of us to endure the worst of days to gain a better perspective on those who did experience the "better angels of our nature," to quote Lincoln. We must be willing to share the story and those who need to hear must be willing to listen.

Those days, when we get our "being human" *right*, we can at least partly answer the questions that have so often been asked of me since that September day in 2001. How did this group of fire alarm dispatchers find their way through that day to not just answer the calls but coordinate the response? What happens after such a catastrophic event? What motivated, inspired, and supported my journey to join that group and spend such an important portion of my life so far away from where it had begun or where I thought I was headed professionally or personally? What insights about the people, organization, and events I experienced can I offer for people and organizations during these crazy times in which we find ourselves today?

This is partly how I framed that point in 2016.

> "From the women and men, I was so blessed to serve with comes an equally important lesson: commitment. Whether you were a firefighter climbing the stairs of a burning tower, a paramedic caring for the injured, a police officer helping victims to safety, or a dispatcher easing the last moments of someone trapped with no way out, each person gave their all for someone, for a stranger, for their community. They did what had to be done, even though they could not imagine, truly, what that would mean.
>
> "On that particular day, we lost three-hundred forty-three firefighters, thirty-seven port authority police officers, twenty-three NYPD members, and eight EMS personnel. In the years that have followed, we have lost many more to cancer, to the aftereffects of physical injuries, and to the emotional scars that just wouldn't heal.
>
> "Today is, in many ways, a day to honor those brave and loving souls. But I would also like to challenge you to remember and share the even greater lessons of that day. We are all in this together. We all need each other.
>
> "History, especially that of events like 9/11, must not be something we store in the attic, only to pull out on holidays or when distant relatives visit. History serves its best purpose when we live with it, acknowledge its lessons, and accept

that it provides important insights to who and how we are today—and who and how we must be tomorrow."

Occasionally, those lessons and miracles are best seen in the pitch-black darkness of a city with no lights.

2 | THE BLACKOUT OF AUGUST 2003

Sometimes, especially in a city, you can feel something is very wrong, even if you don't know what it is. There is a sense from the people around you, a commotion or a murmur. Sometimes the noise is just off. Maybe it's louder than normal, or perhaps quieter. Maybe it's a smell—something out of place in the normal environment. One thing about being in a city of over eight million people is a collective sensation, a general mood that provides hints of things and permeates your daily life. A "vibe," if you will, that affects everything around you. I imagine it's similar to the feeling a parent or teacher has when she or he can sense that someone is up to something that just is not right. A similar sensation is developed when you choose a career in public safety as a dispatcher. You are consistently forced to make decisions about critical things with very little information. What responses are the highest in priority? What is the actual location of an emergency? Is this event more serious than the person perhaps reported? So many questions and answers from a simple phone call that lasts only a few seconds, followed by several dispatchers applying their instincts, intuition and knowledge to whatever the caller reported. A phone call where a person under significant stress shares information that combines with your personal experience and that of your fellow dispatchers to create an initial picture of the event being reported. Until the first fire department apparatus arrives, it is that picture and your decisions that guide the actions of the department and can have very serious consequences.

There are not unlimited resources. The busier the shift, the less resources there are to go around, managing those resources is an art form that takes years of experience to learn how to do effectively. Doing that for hours at a time nearly every day leads to a life where you get quick impressions of things and then act, or at least hopefully plan out what you should do. That proved true when I made it to the street after getting ready for my work shift on an August afternoon in 2003. I knew when I made it outside my apartment building that something might be off. There were far too many people on the street for a normal afternoon and the noise of the traffic and the honking cars was well beyond typical for my quiet, by New York standards, section of Brooklyn. I did, however, fail to notice there was no power in the neighborhood. It was a bright day and, thanks to having more windows than the typical New York City apartment and a pretty simple work preparation routine, I did not need any artificial lights to get ready for work.

Although the crowds on the street were large, it was late summer—prime outside time in the city—so even that was not particularly strange. Nevertheless, there was a noticeable "chatter" that I did not fully process for a few more minutes. It is fair to say that, at times, I suffer from being particularly focused on my mission. On this day, my mission was to arrive for the night tour at the FDNY Queens Central Office on Woodhaven Boulevard. It would be a long trip, but if I made it to the subway by 5:00 p.m., I would get to the office around 6:30 p.m. This was not as early as I would like, but decent for someone who relied on public transit to get around the city.

It was not until I hit the last step on the descent into the subway station at Bay Ridge Avenue that I truly appreciated the situation. It was dark—pitch black in a place that was normally bathed in the hues of the incandescent lights of the MTA. There was a train conductor who was not on a train, but standing on the mezzanine level of the station with a radio squawking out instructions for all train operators and conductors to secure their trains. That was when it truly hit me: blackout—the type of once-in-a-generation event that fills the journals of New York history with stories of horror, heroism, chaos, and confusion.

There had been at least two major Blackouts before, in 1965 and 1977. The 1977 version was the focus of countless documentaries and news stories due to occurring right in the middle of the infamous "Summer of Sam" killing spree, a World Series Run by the New York Yankees, and the "Bronx is Burning" phase of New York History. The "Bronx is Burning" was a decade long period of extreme amounts of fire activity across the city and especially in the South Bronx. The stories of that time had been some of my earliest introductions to the FDNY when I read the famous (in the fire service) book "Report from Engine Company 82" by FDNY firefighter Dennis Smith in my early twenties around the time I made my first brief New York City trip. That book had further opened my eyes to the craziness and camaraderie that was central to the FDNY as well as its legacy of culture, tradition, and commitment. With the stories of the intense shifts of work from that book as well as my own dispatching experiences in FDNY from multiple crazy days including September 11th running through my mind, I started to contemplate what managing such an event would mean for the shift I was supposed to be leading in Queens, which was now a seemingly impossible distance away. I made my way back up the stairs to the street, thinking I would take the bus to the Brooklyn Central Office and then figure out how to make it the rest of the way to Queens. Maybe the blackout would be over by then. Perhaps the department could arrange transportation. Either way, getting to someplace work-related was better than facing a blackout on the streets of Brooklyn. Oh, and one other thing: whether in Brooklyn or Queens, work would have air conditioning, and that was no small thing! Each of the FDNY Central Offices boasted twin generators that would ensure a cool environment for the technology and equipment in the buildings and, thankfully, for the dispatchers working in them.

August was always a challenging month in New York City. The air was hot, the buildings were hot, and the people were hot. It was a difficult place to navigate in the best of times, and the soup of heat and humidity and lack of patience that marked the dog days of summer made nothing easier. Many people escaped from New York to the Hamptons or upstate in the hottest summer months; I was not one of those people. I was living in a typical Brooklyn apartment by this point. It was a small, first-floor, one-bedroom unit on the edge of Bay Ridge, which would be my home neighborhood for the duration of my time in the city.

The variety of people who lived within a couple of blocks of my place was unimaginable in almost any other part of the United States. There were Puerto Ricans on my block and the largest mosque in New York City around the corner. Jewish, Italian, and Chinese enclaves were within a five-minute walk. All of these areas surrounded a neighborhood started as a Nordic immigrant enclave over a hundred years ago. In New York City, one clue of how a neighborhood began is the names of its parks. The closest to me was named Leif Erikson, after the explorer history considers the first to make it to North America. (Sorry, Christopher Columbus.) However, neither Chris nor Erik would have felt at ease in the place that was my home and certainly not in facing the initial moments of a historic event. Between the teeming crowds and the diverse make-up of the population, the area had changed a great deal from one hundred years prior. For me and millions of others in New York City and the entire Northeastern United States and Eastern Canada, this blackout would quickly become another "once-in-a-career moment" and a reminder of the best of what this generation of dispatchers and members of the FDNY could accomplish.

Thankfully, New Yorkers, both within the public safety realm and in the general public, are a resilient bunch. They were still holding close the reminders and echoes of their 9/11 experiences when the lights went out. For most New Yorkers, 9/11 served as a reminder of the power of coming together in crisis. One thing New York City teaches you quite quickly is that to hate other people for something other than their actual behavior is a luxury that cannot stand. All those different people are, in fact, essential, and you cannot know when that essential nature will surface. It may be the Chinese owners of the corner store who let you pay them later when you forget your wallet. It may be the Chinese owners of the best neighborhood Mexican restaurant who always add an extra tortilla. It may be the Greek diner owner's brother who is full of side-splitting stories when you are eating chicken fingers and drinking a chocolate shake at 3:00 a.m., recovering from another attempted blind date gone horribly, disastrously wrong.

It's all about the stew of community that each neighborhood represents. Even when a particular neighborhood features one predominant population, that group of people is only a block or two away from another distinctive collection of people. It makes New York crushingly stressful at times, but also, like a good stew, rich and filling, complex and sublime. No days expressed that more clearly than the intensely challenging ones, especially September 11, 2001, and the blackout of 2003. This is not to say that all was easy or that every person lived up to their Richard Scarry Busytown potential. For the most part, the big scary days were, first and foremost, a shock to the system that forced everyone to remember we were all in this together.

At that point in my career, my job was to lead a small team of FDNY dispatchers as a shift (or tour) supervisor. FDNY Fire Alarm Dispatchers, working in each of the five Central or Communications Offices (CO's) were responsible for answering and processing fire department calls for service and a variety of related tasks. Those additional tasks ranged from ensuring adequate fire resource coverage to helping maintain the system of Fire Boxes that can be found on street corners throughout New York City. A relic of sorts from a bygone age before the advent of cell phones, but in many ways a vital communications tool in the face of modern disasters, like blackouts when those cell phones and their networks frequently and quickly run out of power.

A strange combination of events, five years of previous fire dispatch experience from my time in Ohio, a college degree, and a lack of other willing applicants led me to provisional promotion in January of 2003. Being a provisional meant I would have to do well on an upcoming test to keep my job. I would also constantly be last on the seniority list, which would happen anyway, given my limited time on the job when I was promoted. I had wavered about taking the promotion. I felt like I had a lot of personal and professional growing up to do given that the historical norm for time on the job for promotion was five to ten years, and I had only lived in New York for just under three years at that point. Nevertheless, I was prompted by senior members who had more faith in me than I did, and I was selected.

My first assignment was in our Queens dispatch office, where I was responsible for a tour of people more senior on the job than I was by decades. I was the young, hotshot supervisor tasked with leading some of the most infamous characters in FDNY fire dispatch operations history. They ranged from the inscrutable former NYPD Dispatcher and cab driver who was a master chef and brilliant radio dispatcher to a former country musician with anger management issues, but a heart of gold hidden under the aftereffects of years of public safety service to the city of New York. They were all very experienced, with strong ideas about the way they wanted to do the job. Their ways had been established long before I arrived and my desire to do even minor tweaks, such as improving our call-answer times, was met with a decent amount of resistance. Those ideas sometimes (or often) conflicted with my ideas about what to do and how to do it. Needless to say, my thoughts about change and improving their performance met the harsh reality of a team of dedicated and experienced public servants. They were quite happy to keep doing what they were doing the way they were doing it, thank you very much. After all, I was a brand-new supervisor without a permanent assignment. That role, defined as "covering," meant I could be moved somewhere else with minimal notice. It's very hard to get a team to buy into how you want to do things when the system sets you up to be perceived as a temporary solution. The shift was also processing the recent departure of their long-term supervisor due to medical reasons. They did not know if he was coming back in a few weeks, or ever. In retrospect, it was probably not fair for me to expect any changes in their performance until they knew I was going to be working with them for a while. Until that was the case, I was just going to be the FDNY Fire Dispatch equivalent of a substitute teacher.

It was an eye-opening, crazy experience for me learning just how much change I could make happen (very little) and how to make it happen (very slowly). No matter what, I always made sure to get the payroll right, and the journal completed which were the two primary roles of a supervisor. Payroll even in 2003 was a manual process involving carbon sheets and handwritten reports, which were supported by the entries in the line journal book in which all the activities of the shift were recorded in either red, blue, or black ink

This only scratches the surface of a period of learning I still reflect on with embarrassed pride. They put up with it and with me, and, in time, we became a very good team. I learned more than I could ever give justice to in the time I was with them. The most important lesson was that even though they were not regarded as a super star team, they had experience and wisdom about the job and the city and how to make things work that they did not always display. But it was there. On the hard days—with multiple fires, major accidents, or serious weather—they would magically find a mode of operation that ensured the job got done. Being at work with them on those days was truly a pleasure, and it could be said that was where I learned how to be a supervisor. I had slowly begun to figure out the important place of mutual trust in effective supervision, that others could do things differently than I would and still be effective, and that I had found a place in the FDNY that felt somewhat like home.

That was why, even though the subway trip on a normal day was about ninety minutes over two or three lines plus a fifteen-minute walk up the hill to the office, I never minded at all the assignment or the journey. Now, facing a nearly impossible task of getting all the way to Queens without aid of the subway, it became all about making it five miles to the Brooklyn Central Office. I had started my career there just under three years before, and it was my closest physical point of connection to FDNY Fire Dispatch Operations.

In retrospect, I should have realized the bus would not be the most efficient way to travel. The streetlights were out, there were crowds at every crosswalk, and everyone else had the same idea. I only made it about ten blocks up Fifth Avenue into Sunset Park before I gave up and walked off the bus into the masses. I committed myself to a humid, hot four plus mile walk from 60th Street to the east side of Prospect Park, where the Brooklyn Central Office stood. This managed to make it more quickly than I expected. Time spent exploring the city helped me navigate the way around the gothic beauty of Green-Wood Cemetery, up Fort Hamilton Parkway to the edge of Prospect Park. That was when I realized I was about to pass out from thirst and the initial phases of heat stroke. Thankfully, there was a firehouse nearby and I managed to drag myself to the front doors of Engine Company 240 and the 48th Battalion. I can only imagine how bad I looked. They gave me water with minimal explanation, and the battalion chief offered to give me a ride to the other side of the park. I made it into the office just a little before 7:00 p.m. to a group of dispatchers, supervisors, and a chief dispatcher doing their best possible work in that day's challenging conditions.

The various side effects of people living without power meant more medical incidents, more fires, more of everything. The Computer Assisted Dispatch (CAD) system which we used to do our job suffered as well, everything slowing down until it became more effective to process this incredible volume of incidents the old-fashioned way—manually and largely by hand. With skill, knowledge, and a series of manual processes that tied back to the origin of FDNY dispatching in 1855, we ended up managing the deluge of incidents associated with the blackout. As crazy as that may sound, the entire experience proved to be my favorite time ever at work. Operating as part of a well-oiled team as they did what they do best was euphoric. This was particularly true while watching the senior Brooklyn dispatcher manage the deployment of units to incidents off the top of his head in constant sync with the rest of the team. Along with this was the churn of units leaving alarms only to be immediately dispatched by radio to their next assignment, based on overheard phone calls, insight about street networks, and pure intuition. This was where a team of dispatchers working together were able to demonstrate the power of knowing their borough, understand the insight to be gained from a caller's tone of voice or the words she or he were using to report a fire. Not all reports of fires are the same, especially during busy periods. "I smell a little smoke in the basement" is an entirely different situation than "I see fire coming out three windows of the house across the street." That same degree of potential seriousness can also be found in the location that is being reported. The Empire State Building on foggy nights, for example, exudes a fog that for many people looks like smoke—and sometimes they call 911 to report it. Certain areas of the city almost never experience fires, so getting even a single call from those neighborhoods reporting a fire is cause for concern. Multiple calls reporting a fire almost always significantly elevates the amount of attention that dispatchers will give an incident and potentially the amount of fire companies being assigned to it.

During the blackout I staffed the decision dispatcher position, which serves as ringmaster for the entire operation, coordinating the information received from both the public and field units and ensuring that adequate resources are assigned to each event. I supported the radio dispatcher and ensured that highest priority events were handled in a timely manner. During periods of such significant activity, the highest priority events were those with a clear threat to life. Incidents that were not as serious, like outside fires or event fires in vacant buildings, might be stacked further down in the queue of incidents we were processing. Normally this position would be worked by a dispatcher and not a supervisor, but owing to my familiarity with Brooklyn and my ability to work through the manual processes that served as our way through the quagmire, I eagerly accepted my role while I waited for whatever assignment would come next.

Every desk in the office was staffed, including some extras, meaning there was a constant barrage of new emergencies, changing unit statuses, updates from incidents, and procedural adjustments to make the best use of our maxed-out fire department resources. Every one of these actions was tracked manually on a very complex status board in the center of the floor where each company was represented by a multi-colored plastic chip. Each incident was set up in a row of vertical slots. You could tell almost anything about a unit by how and where it was positioned on the board. The board sort of resembled the "Plinko" game from *The Price is Right*, especially if a chip would accidentally slide down the board.

It was complete and total bedlam but it never, ever got loud or out of hand. It was managed chaos that can only be compared to what the floor of the New York Stock Exchange used to look like before computers, technology, AI, and everything else largely replaced the chaos and charm with an orderly, boring hum. The team knew what it was doing because the processes and procedures were so well defined. Because the dispatchers on the floor knew their jobs and what was expected of them, what would appear to outsiders to be a crushing circus of insanity was actually a fully functional and quite effective tempest in a teapot. It was remarkable to be a part of it all.

I expected ultimately to be transported to the Queens Dispatch Office that evening to join my normal team. An hour or two in, however, the chief dispatcher came out to tell me I would have a different destination. The deputy director for dispatch operations drove me and another dispatcher to our Manhattan communications office. The drive through the blacked-out streets of New York was beyond surreal. Lights and sirens blaring, we slowly made our way up Flatbush Avenue through crowds of people, then over the Manhattan Bridge up the East Side Highway. Everywhere, people were on the streets, just hanging out. Our journey did not pass looting or riots, just thousands of New Yorkers on a hot, dark, summer night hanging out with their neighbors and wondering, like all of us, when the lights would come back on.

Upon walking into the Manhattan Central Office, it was clear this was going to be an entirely different beast. It was not the fault of the personnel. The complete and total inundation of incidents and responses made perfect sense when you consider what Manhattan is: the "high-rise" part of New York City. It is only twenty-three square miles, but over 1.5 million inhabitants, visitors, and workers. As a result of the blackout, hundreds of elevators were stuck with people in them, many having increasingly severe breathing difficulties. There were fires in high-rise buildings and a multitude of other emergencies on the street in process. It was an almost overwhelming professional experience, but it lacked the smoothness, grace, and effectiveness of the operation in Brooklyn. The geography of Manhattan, a long, narrow island where it is historically challenging to have emergency units move across town because of the street and traffic patterns, made the situation worse. It was also very difficult to borrow units from other boroughs, given that they were all busy themselves. It developed into a chess match of prioritization, doing the best we could with what we had to work with, sometimes with limited results.

Several hours in, we were able to secure food delivery from a local restaurant. I took a moment to scarf down a chicken sandwich only to realize two bites in that the only part of the sandwich that had actually been cooked was the first bite and maybe a small bit of the second. There would be no third bite. The rest of the shift, which would slow and pause as though the entire island of Manhattan took a smoke break, then picked up again with full vigor and chaotic rage, featured fires, more rescues, and very little food. The following morning, a fellow supervisor was kind enough to give me a ride home to Brooklyn on his way to Staten Island. The sun was up by then, and power was returning to selected sections of the city.

Like the aftermath of the 1977 blackout, our drive back through the city featured the sight of smoke rising from multiple fires. The city felt like it had been pushed, tested, and challenged by yet another hard day but had miraculously survived. It was a reminder of September 11, 2001, in some ways but completely different in others. Thankfully, there wasn't a horrible loss of life and there would be relatively little national attention, owing to a lack of a crazed populace looting and burning sections of the city. A community coming together to overcome something challenging and doing so in a largely non-dramatic way just was not news. Even the fires were relatively low-key as fires go. All in all, the team I was so lucky to be part of and the city I was blessed to be a resident of had weathered the blackout well.

When I made it back to my apartment, it was a different feeling than after 9/11. It was one of pride and belonging. It is what I imagine winning a sports championship would feel like. I knew I was part of a team that exceeded expectations and needed the contributions of every team member to succeed. I had some breakfast and, after winding down for a bit, managed to go to sleep. I was due back in the Queens Central Office for a night shift that evening. Before I fell asleep, I thought for a bit about all that had taken place in my time in New York and as part of the fire department. I had jotted down several pages of notes in the momentary lulls that happened during the shift working the Blackout in Manhattan, and I knew that the shift had offered an unmistakable opportunity to learn. That's what it was all about in the big picture. I did not know fully then where the journey would take me. I certainly did not know what would happen with my job in the coming years. However, I knew I was there, in New York City, a part of the world's greatest fire department. I had worked through some of the craziest days imaginable and even one that was completely, thoroughly unimaginable.

My God, I asked myself, *how had that all happened? What had brought me to that crazy place in those crazy days and what was I expected to take from it?* Yes, my time in New York City and even my path to getting to New York was full of miracles. It was also full of a great many challenges and days where, given the chance, I would have crawled my way back home to Ohio—but I didn't. That opportunity never presented itself and I fought through. The fighting or the miracles or the turning points that could have led me in entirely different directions did not start when I arrived in New York City. Like most people, my experience in New York was heavily influenced by events that had taken place long before I was born. A menagerie of miracle and tragedy, decision, and regret by loved ones and strangers alike had started a process that, on that August morning, saw me riding home to Brooklyn after one of the most eventful shifts I could ever imagine.

Of course, I was not thinking about all of that at the time. I was in the awake-coma phase of recovery from a crazy shift, appreciating being home and having electrical power, which by that point had returned to my neighborhood in Brooklyn. I did think, too, about how far I had come from being a little boy who grew up loving visits to the firehouse, dreaming of the big city, and eager to be a part of something bigger. Well, here I was—mission accomplished. It had only been three years since I arrived in New York and became a part of the FDNY Bureau of Communications. It had only been a few months since I was promoted to supervisor. Although so much was new, to be a part of another crazy event was just one more step in a process. A process of miracles and milestones had led me to New York, to a career I did not even recognize was going to be almost permanent, and experiences that were beyond my control—or even my imagination.

3 THE EARLY YEARS

The combination of fate and circumstances that could be labeled miraculous started years before my arrival in New York. My mother Shirely and father Jack were high-school sweethearts. As an only child who loved stories before falling asleep, I eagerly listened to the story of how my parents met, what life was like for my mother on the farm where she grew up, and the circumstances that led to me being in their lives. I never had a day when I did not know I was adopted, and I do not recall not knowing at least the shared version of the circumstances behind my parents making that choice. I feel a ripple of sadness for those who do not find out until later in life the truth of their birth story. I can only imagine that shock completely flipping life as they know it upside down. That was never me. I grew up celebrating the unconventional way I started out, giggling when classmates in elementary school would tell me I looked like my dad and then being offended beyond measure when people asked if I wanted to find my "real" parents. I was surprisingly young when I formulated the snap-back response of "Aren't my real parents the ones I actually live with?" I took it as a badge of honor and a cause of celebration that I was special and different and the product of a process that was not ordinary. That does not mean that my biological parents should be ignored. I regret that today I cannot say much about them. It's a fair guess that they could have been college lovers based on what little I know about their ages and history. I know they were nineteen years old when I was born and at some point, before or after that moment, they made a decision that was courageous and heart wrenching. They gave up their newborn son for adoption.

What I also know is that when I arrived, I was quickly placed in the care of Franklin County Children's Services. I would remain in their charge for the first two months of my life, living with foster parents who were, by all accounts, extremely loving and kind. That impression is based on letters they wrote to my adoptive parents to give them advance insight into the child they were waiting to adopt officially. The foster family provided detailed descriptions of my behaviors, what I enjoyed doing, and my general personality. Even at a few weeks old, I enjoyed watching the news, stayed up late, and only stopped crying when held by men. As they say, some things never change. Neither the lack of information about my biological parents nor letters from my foster parents offered clues into the weaving, wandering path that would lead me years later to the streets of America's largest city. At some subconscious level, I have no doubt my biological and foster parents left an impression. I often feel a tug of connection to them I cannot fully describe to someone. Those moments whisper from across that biological tether and the distance created by decisions and choices. Those moments remind me that my story is not simply linear. I cannot draw my line distinctly and completely back from who and where I am to who and what I was without acknowledging the mysterious influences of people who I will never know. Sure, some of it is physical. I have the allergies of my biological family and a few other health issues described in my paperwork. I also have feelings of abandonment from time to time, of being disconnected from a part of myself and a part of my story, and an alternate path that was there but not taken.

Therefore, I am, at my very core, an adaptation. I am a blending of a life that could have been, and an alternate one offered to me without my knowledge. Studies suggest that there are lingering consequences from being separated from your birth family. I tend to believe them, especially when looking back and seeing my need for connection, my need for approval, and my need to be wanted. I have found those things most assuredly in my "real" family, where I would be joined by an unexpected, but much celebrated sister in 1981. I have no complaints to be sure, but it is also fair to acknowledge that love and longing come in many forms. Even in the face of great gifts and wonders, we can still feel other feelings. A dad who saved me from choking on a Lifesaver when I was three would later say he would rather have a dead son than a gay one. A mother who firmly believed that I was going to be president one day lovingly piled on the pressure of expectations that would nearly break me as I tried to be the perfect son, live up to my "gifted child" label, and overcome my existence as a gay person in times and places where that was not as accepted as it is today

Their stories and those of their families explain much of how I ended up where I did. Children of Depression-era parents, my mother and father went to high school together in rural southern Ohio. My dad was one of multiple children born to Walter and Agnes near the town of McDermott and on the same road where, a generation before, the cowboy actor known as Roy Rogers had been born and raised as Leonard Franklin Slye. Agnes was Walter's second wife, and in a testament to the customs of Appalachia at the time, she was a young teenager when they married after the passing of his first wife. They would have multiple children together, including my father in 1944. By the time they stopped having children, several had been lost to childhood illnesses or car accidents. Later, at least one would be lost to the demons of alcoholism and hopelessness. My mom's upbringing was completely the opposite. An only child born to a very stable set of parents, considered upstanding members of the community, she was doted on and spoiled on their one-hundred-sixty-acre farm near Otway, about thirteen air miles from where my dad was raised in an environment best described as hard-scrabble and which may as well have been a thousand miles away in real terms. Mom's father, George, was a farmer and fiddle player with, by all accounts, a gregarious personality beloved by family and friends.

Mom's mother, Lenora, was a gifted pianist who survived a bout of polio but still retained an "Auntie Mame" approach to life. She was always up for adventure and road trips and driving quickly in the hills of Southern Ohio in a white early 1970s Ford Tornio.

My mother and father met while in high school and, after a few relationship stops and starts, married in 1964. After marrying, they settled in the Columbus, Ohio suburb of Whitehall. Their first apartment was near Town and Country Shopping Center, one of the first shopping centers in America designed and intended for people on the move by automobile. My dad was soon employed at the Ohio Department of Agriculture, Mom at a bank. So began their efforts to build a life and family. Their quest to have their first child was interrupted by the United States Army when Dad was drafted to service in Vietnam. The photos of my dad from the family photo album are striking. They represent before and after Vietnam, or before and after hope in his future, or before and after innocence. To think that someone could go through an event as traumatic as war and not be permanently affected is nonsense.

After he returned home, one element of their new life continued to offer challenges and stress. My mom was not able to carry a child successfully. Facing the prospect of never having children biologically, they decided in 1970 to put themselves on an adoption waiting list with Franklin County Children's Services.

After my mother and father married and moved north, my maternal grandparents, George and Lenora, were forced to find new outlets for the energy they had previously focused on their only child. The result was a flurry of traveling and social engagements that filled multiple photo albums. They continued to farm, and they played music. They were full participants in the lives of their extended family, which involved the "adoption" of the neighbor kids, including the four children of a family who lived just up Mount Hope Road from George and Lenora's farm.

It was while transporting the four kids of a neighboring family to a picnic at Lake White near Wavery, Ohio on May 11, 1974, that a Mead Paper Company truck, headed south on US 23, blew a tire. The out-of-control truck careened across the median and smashed head-on into my grandparent's car. My grandfather died instantly. My grandmother and two of the children were severely injured. Grandma would spend the next several months in a hospital in Columbus, where the physical injuries slowly healed while she tried to process the loss of her husband. Although the two injured children would largely recover, they would forever suffer side effects from the accident. For my mother, the loss of a parent was terribly hard, especially as an only child at the young age of twenty-nine. I would come to know a version of that experience as well, finding out that losing a parent at thirty is not much easier.

In the middle of moving Grandmother back to the farm in September, after her long hospital stay, that the phone rang one late summer afternoon. My mother answered to hear an unfamiliar voice asking for either Shirley or Jack Carver. I wonder if my Mom and Dad had fully given up their dream of parenthood or if they were unexpectedly shocked by the words coming from the other end of the receiver. "This is Franklin County Children's Services. If you are still interested in adopting, we have the most amazing, wonderful, awesome child for you." That statement might be a bit embellished, but you get the point. The time had come for my parents to become parents! On a sad, broken day at the end of a sad, broken time, they had been given the greatest gift they could imagine. My dad had been out in the woods with the dogs when the call came, and my mother, after composing herself, ran out to try to find him to tell him the good news. Not being able to track him down, she decided to sound the horn on the car. She did so continuously until Dad realized something was up. The reaction of Dad, and Mom, and still recovering Grandma to the news must have been indescribable.

The process of taking home a child is not, however, immediate. The steps to bringing home your newly adopted child required weeks or months of court proceedings, reviews, visits, and various types of preparation, as well as a not-so-clear timeline.

On a wintry November afternoon, my parents got "the call" that it was time to come get me. That call came about a week before it was expected. Not wanting to delay the opportunity, they picked me up from the designated exchange point and turned back toward home on icy roads and freeways. Only on the return trip did they realize that they had no formula, no diapers, or any of the essential supplies required to support a newly arrived infant. The result was a frantic stop at the Harts Department store just before closing. My mother sprinted inside to explain to the manager that she had just had a baby that she was not expecting and begged them to keep the store open so she could get supplies. In what was likely more a reflection of a practical desire to get out of work on time than a heroic mission to support a new mother, the entire workforce of the store fanned out with shopping carts to get all the items my parents would need to take care of the early arriving son. I have often wondered what the store employees thought when she said the arrival was unexpected. It always made a better story to just leave it and accept that from my first arrival in the city of Reynoldsburg, success was going to be a group effort and that miracles sometimes (most of the time) arrive with little warning and almost never according to plan.

From that moment on, I settled into the spoiled, idyllic life of an adopted only child in a suburb as Norman Rockwell could have illustrated for a Saturday Evening Post cover. Living adjacent to a court (or cul-de-sac), our split-level house featured the furnishings and décor standard for the mid-1970s and ample opportunities for outdoor fun. Gold shag carpeting? Check. Sputnik-style clock? Check. Green couch? Check. Huffy bike? Absolutely! It was all there, and I fell into it with as much enthusiasm as I could muster. That included exploring the nearby woods and not-yet-developed farmland that would eventually become a Kmart store and adjacent branch of the public library.

Along the way, something else developed: a realization that I was not exactly the most normal of children.

I loved to read, not just picture books but newspapers and current affairs magazines from the age of about four. I strived to be self-sufficient and to learn. I loved maps most of all. My dad's role with the state of Ohio had evolved, and he was now on the road most of the time. It was fascinating to me to follow where my dad's work travels took him. These were not to exotic locations of other countries or even different states, of course. No, the world I followed on the state maps that hung on my bedroom walls was fully contained in the eighty-eight counties of Ohio—places like Cadiz and Chardon, Pomeroy, and Defiance. I would learn as much as I could about those places. In time, I expanded my focus and wanted to learn as much about the rest of the world as I could, *National Geographic Magazine* and Rand McNally road atlases were gateway drugs that formed a social science-focused curiosity that has never abated.

I devoured the news with the ferocity most children reserve for candy. I wanted to understand how the world worked and what the events I read about meant. I also read a crazy amount of history for a kid in the first grade and the news for me was like a window into the creation of history in real time. An early highlight was my first-grade teacher providing leftover copies of the local paper for me to read on weekends. There were books, too, and *Sesame Street* and *Mister Rogers' Neighborhood* on PBS, and too much time in the library. One children's author stoked a love of diversity and community: Richard Scarry. The Busytown books with Postman Pig and the wildly creative and energetic life depicted in see-through buildings that hinted at the wonder and creativity behind every door were highly compelling. When you combined that with the kindness and wonder of Mister Rogers and the "friends that you meet walking down your street" menagerie of *Sesame Street*, I suppose the result was inevitable. Relocating to New York not so many years later was probably the least surprising thing ever considering just how many photos of cities were on my walls and just how many *National Geographic* articles on different places, culture, and people I had consumed.

4 | AWAKENINGS

When my teenage years began, I had one great love above all others: airplanes. I truly loved airplanes. My second love was history. When I was six or seven, a friend of my dad strapped me into the back of a Piper Cub at Newark Heath Airport, and I was off. From that moment on, I wanted to fly more than anything. I was convinced my future would involve traveling the world as a pilot, possibly for the military. I bought and read every book I could find about aviation, as well as history, especially World War II. One of my essential research tools was a World War II encyclopedia gifted to me by my grandmother. It was an invaluable tool for looking up people and places I learned about in World War II movies or documentaries.

At my first "real" job behind the counter of a drug store in Columbus, Ohio, I had the sneaking suspicion that the kind, quiet, elderly gentleman coming in regularly to fill prescriptions was someone I should know. Something motivated me to look him up in that World War II encyclopedia. On the pages I discovered that once a week or so, I engaged in brief small talk with and handed a simple paper sack of medicine to the pilot of the *Enola Gay*, Paul Tibbets. Not only did we interact at the Drug Store, but later when I moved to working at a local camera shop, he would come there as well to get film developed and, at least once, to buy a new camera. We did not talk extensively about the specifics of his military service, but I did get to know him. He was as unassuming a person as you could imagine. I can't even recall what his voice sounded like, but I enjoyed just being in his presence. He reminded me of my love for history, and aviation and inspired me with his approach. He offered important insights about leadership and teamwork through his demeanor and our discussions. My research into his mission as a bomb wing commander only furthered my respect for his service. In our few talks we did have about his role in the war, he focused on his duty—on doing the job he was tasked with as a member of the military and as a pilot. You could tell he was a committed person, even in his advancing years. There was no flair or bravado, just a focus on doing what he was called to do. That approach would stick with me and help formulate many of my own principles when I was promoted into positions of supervision.

Sadly, a few years before I met Colonel Tibbets, my dream of being a military pilot crashed and burned. In sixth grade, my vision went from 20/20 to 20/400 and with it any possibility of a military flying career. For whatever reason, I did not adapt or consider other aviation-related possibilities, such as flying commercially or becoming an air traffic controller. It would be safe to say I never again found something I was so certain that I wanted to do with my life.

What did become clear, if not on the career side of life, was the "where" side of my future. It took a while for me to circle back to my Richard Scarry-inspired goal of living in an urban environment, but that desire was enduring and real. The taste of living in community had been cemented by knowing the neighbors, the people at the library and the stores, and at church. The feeling of being a part of something, anything, was more powerful than any specific job title. That, in retrospect, made me a prime candidate for the paramilitary organizational environment of the fire service and the high-performing team world of 9/11.

In the quest to find my path forward and stay somewhat engaged with aviation, I asked my parents for a specific gift for my fifteenth birthday. A Regency HX1500 handheld scanner allowed me to listen to all kinds of cool radio transmissions, including the airplanes, which I still loved but in a slightly lesser way post eyesight challenges. It was a window into a world that enthralled me with its special language, mission-critical focus, and precision. Although it worked perfectly at the airport, I lived just a bit too far away from the airport to hear much at home, so I had to find other uses for my new device. A trip to the local Radio Shack would change my life.

There, I purchased the latest edition of *Police Call*, a publication of radio frequencies, radio ten-codes, and other information intended to support the community of people who enjoyed listening to radio traffic. I quickly found the frequencies for the local fire departments and programmed them into the scanner. Although the radio frequencies were initially quiet, within a few moments the trajectory of my life had changed courtesy of a tone and a radio dispatch message.

The first fire incident I heard through the scanner's speaker was the Columbus Fire Department dispatching Engine-7 to High Street and Euclid Avenue for a Winnebago camper on fire. I was hooked in an instant. Memories of years spent watching reruns of TV shows like *Adam-12* and *Emergency*, my early trips to the firehouse with my Dad, and my love of this adventurous and exciting world bloomed into a blazing passion.

I decided to learn everything I could about the world I had just stumbled into: the codes, the fire station locations, the apparatus. All of it was there for me to explore. A love for the fire service and the art of dispatching and communications had become my sole focus.

I joined local radio clubs and fire buff organizations. I connected with fellow enthusiasts who would become mentors. They taught me everything about being a good dispatcher and the critical role that command, control, and communications played. A good dispatcher was clearly defined as someone who could multi-task, manage complex operational challenges, who knew about fire operations and, seemingly, who could tell a great story. Skills with maps and geography were also essential, as was the ability to be calm and effective in a crisis. A retired Columbus fire lieutenant who had been assigned to their fire department dispatch office was one of the most important of my new buddies. We had been introduced by a mutual friend who was involved in a fire department "buff" group in Central Ohio. This club of about 20 individuals interested in the fire service would meet and share stories from their trips to New York, Chicago, Buffalo and other cities rich in fire department tradition. I would visit his house and hang out in the basement decorated with fire department memorabilia and a functional fire telegraph bell system. I listened to war stories about firefighting and dispatching. In an advantageous twist of fate, his childhood best friend had left Columbus to pursue a career in government and the military. He had become an honorary chief with the Fire Department of the City of New York. He had authored an extensive book about FDNY operations and procedures and later became an important supporter in my efforts to be hired in that organization.

It became clear to me from listening to radio traffic and learning from mentors that to be in the dispatch office was to be a member of a mission-critical orchestra where each person had a role to play. The team environment was much more a fire department attribute than EMS, where you would generally work with only one other person, or law enforcement where the entire mindset was completely different and almost individualistic. Fires were complex, interesting, and involved a collection of skills and attributes that appealed to things I was already interested in. The sum of it all was much more significant than its parts. Another friend, who would later help me to get my first dispatch job, became my Friday or Saturday night adventure buddy. We would drive around the city, going to any fires that came in, but most of all exploring different neighborhoods and stopping to visit firehouses where we were warmly received and got to know many members of local fire departments. There were others, too, and this collection of fire buffs provided me, yet again, with a very important experience of community. Above all, the Fire Service and my group of people offered me my first chance to be a part of something bigger than myself—and something like acceptance.

Critically, this community had also given me something else valuable: a distraction. Many other "normal" high school aged boys would be out dating on weekends, going to the mall, or the arcade, or just hanging at friends' houses. Those were places I did not feel welcomed or included and, increasingly, I was pretty certain I knew why.

5 | AVOIDANCE

It was 1990. I was a kid growing up with Baptist parents, going to a Baptist church, in a Midwestern town, slowly realizing I was gay. Like every other gay kid in my predicament, I sought refuge with a bunch of much older, straight, conservative white guys, often in firehouses. Makes perfect sense, right? I was not an effeminate kid. I never explored any of the behaviors stereotypically associated with being gay. There were never any conversations with my parents about it. It was just something that lived somewhere in the recesses and which I assumed I would just have to hide forever. I had known since first grade what was true. The crush on the kid in another class was as real as any first crush can be. And I knew I did not have the same feelings about the girl in my class that was, in fact, interested in me in that first-grade way.

But given the powers of repression and denial, I was able to avoid the topic of dating altogether until two interesting, and obviously failed, attempts to date girls in high school. In both cases, there was as much energy and connection as in one of those batteries you find way back in the kitchen junk drawer. I knew what was going on. To say I was afraid to admit it to anyone, or even myself, would be a dramatic understatement. I just assumed I would be kicked out of the house and burn in hell for all eternity or, even worse, that I was doomed to be alone. In response, like so many of my generation, I continued to hide who I was and, in some ways, forced myself into the person I was expected to be.

One other outcome was the emphatic decision when I was thirteen not to go to church anymore. I had been going for as long as I could remember. My first church was an interdenominational congregation on the east side of Columbus. After a year or two of going there, my family switched to a Baptist church on the edge of our neighborhood. It would be stereotypical to say that some fire and brimstone anti-gay sermon shook me out of the desire to go, and I never did again, defiant in the face of a lack of acceptance from my faith community. The truth was so much different. Our beloved pastor, who had to have been seventy or older, retired. He was sincere in every aspect of his personality and his ministry. You could see it in his eyes and in every Sunday morning post-church handshake each congregation member received as they walked out of the service. His replacement was not that—not even close. Even to my thirteen-year-old self, he reminded me of a used car salesman. It always felt as though he was trying to sell something polished and new, but far from genuine. If he had given me a Bible I would have suspected it had a rolled back odometer. He never ventured deep into questions or answers, just stayed at the surface of scripture buoyed by the platitudes that too often pass for faith.

As a result, I could no longer see myself going to church. In time, I would come to that same place that so many LGBTQIA+ folks do: my faith forced me to choose between the church and my sexual identity. The truth is I never gave it a chance because I did not feel or know that church was a place I could belong. I was nowhere near confident in myself enough during those years to seek out an open and affirming congregation, and, as a result, simply shut down the spiritual element of my being. I did not feel I could have conversations with my family about it either. It was a very isolated time for me as I navigated my teenage years without a path to answering or even understanding these big-picture questions about who I really was and what my place in the world may be.

I remember telling myself, "I guess I will just never fall in love or have sex then." Having grown up in a Baptist household, the thought of never having sex was not actually far from a real possibility. I think, for whatever reason, I may have assumed that was just the way it went for kids like me. I never recall having a "birds and the bees" conversation with my family or even some sort of angsty teen confession to a trusted friend or confidant. My response was to hide, especially in the context of school.

There was one brave soul in my high school class who was out, or at least the early 1990s version of out. God, was I terrified of him and what he represented. I constructed a belief that if I even talked to him, I would get sucked into a gay vortex, outed, and ostracized, and then it would be game over. I never spoke to him. I did not want to give away any hints, not realizing that my lack of aggressive, hormonally driven dating activities with girls was probably the best indication of all that I was not like the others.

Thankfully, I had a few great friends in and outside of my high school. I was able to find camaraderie and support. Unlike hanging out with fire department friends, with my high school we did geeky dorky stuff like bowling, putt-putt, road trips, and lots of movies. I essentially stayed safe in the bubble world I had created and avoided the drama of romantic relationships

By the time I graduated from high school and picked my college, I had developed a strategy for giving myself space from my family and high school self and maybe even escape from who I was, as well as a plan for seeing the world. From the time I was about ten years old, we had made an annual family pilgrimage to the west coast of Florida to spend time with a great aunt and uncle who lived near Venice. We could get away from the damp, grey, chill that passed for Ohio's weather between late November and early April.

That uncle was my maternal grandmother's brother. He had built a successful career in the insurance industry and managed to have not one but two homes: one in Florida and one in Ohio. He had a magnetic personality of confidence and presence and became a substitute grandparent of sorts after my grandmother's passing in 1984. It seemed logical to follow somewhat in his path and, of course, the weather in Florida was appealing. It would be many years before I realized how much my mother was impacted by the lack of sunlight in Ohio, especially during winter, and the residual side effects of her dreams to travel and explore being deferred by marriage and all that being married entailed. What substituted for her desire to explore the world became our family vacations.

In Venice, Florida, we found one spot that was her favorite on the planet: the jetty, a very narrow outstretched finger into the Gulf of Mexico. The experience of it changed with each step taken toward its end as the smell and sound of the surf changed from beachfront to the ocean's edge. Eventually, at the tip, you could turn back and see the shore, the beaches, and the mauve and pink condo towers and be almost entirely separated from most of the human sounds that accompany a Florida beach. Only the gulls and the surf filled your ears. Occasionally, you would be joined by dolphins or, on the most special of occasions, by a manatee or two. On this narrow split of rock and asphalt, everything else (people, noises, problems, memories) was moon distant. I would realize many years later the allure of a place that allowed you to shut off so much of the world around you. I am happy that my mom managed to find one of those places in her time. I also was never far removed from the understanding that not following your dreams entailed risks, too. Although it was rarely, if ever, discussed, there was always a quality of "what might have been" with my mom. Somehow, understanding that would provide a constant background motivation for me to take leaps at times, especially when it would come to moving to New York City.

A similar longing contributed to my heading to college in Tampa, Florida for the first year and a half of my university career. Where I ended up was not my first choice. That was the historic, urban campus of the University of Tampa, situated on the banks of the Hillsborough River downtown. I went there on a college visit, spent the night in a dorm room, went to a nightclub, and drank very weak Bay Breezes courtesy of a fake ID provided by my gracious hosts. It was heaven on earth, and I was extremely excited to make that my next spot after high school. Sadly, UT did not offer me a full-ride scholarship, and my parents had not adequately prepared to fund a private school for higher education. Therefore, I was forced to settle. The physically nearby, but light years away in everything else, University of South Florida in Tampa, where I had applied as an emergency back-up, offered me an out-of-state tuition waiver, and I accepted. I was happy to be headed south, away, and to someplace that seemed a good fit. The tuition would be affordable as well, and at least it was in Tampa. Tampa was warm, it was away from Ohio, and it offered distance from family that some part of me knew I needed.

I think that within a minute or two of arrival at USF, I realized I had made a terrible mistake. USF at the time was a glorified community college campus with a few dorms and a look and feel right out of the late 1960s institutional architecture of the South. Prison, college, state office building—all had the same feel. There were the mandatory palm trees, the sprawling campus dominated by parking lots and the feeling of being in the exact opposite of the type of school I had wanted to attend. That my obsessed-with-the world self could have entertained for a millisecond the idea of going to college at such a school is probably the best possible testament to how disconnected I was from who I was. The not-quite-so-queer-friendly realities associated with being in the South in 1993 only served as an extra source of confusion about my choice. However, without my time at USF, I would likely have never made it to New York City, or at least not until much later. The experience in Tampa would serve as a springboard to so much of my future life even though, when considered on its own, the experience looks as troubled and pointless as I was convinced it was at the time. That is the point, after all. Life does work in mysterious and misunderstood ways. Even in the aftermath of some of our most questionable choices can be found the starter kits of some of our most wondrous experiences.

Thankfully, and against all odds, my experiences at USF, however short and misguided they were, would bring me into connection with two spheres of influence that profoundly shaped my future life choices. I would probably never have made it to New York on the same timeline without my time among the palmettos. Perhaps equally as important, I may have stayed nailed into the Baptist closet had I not started working for a chain of camera stores at their most unsuccessful location in the entire United States.

After a brief stint at Burger King (three weeks or so) and not wanting to smell like French fries for hours or days after a shift, I took a job selling cameras at a retail outlet in a now-defunct mall on the east side of Tampa. This mall was one of early '80s Florida legacy décor and had a dubious reputation. To battle the frequent crime in the mall, a sheriff's substation was housed in a former storefront. The same substation was burglarized within days of its opening. The Orange Julius, a couple of doors down from our camera shop, was an almost weekly robbery target. In contrast, the jewelry store, electronics stores, and other more logical targets only a few feet away were ignored.

Luckily, the periods of extremely slow activity (the vast majority of the time) were filled with conversation instead of sales. That conversation often involved between the store manager and me. He was likely the first adult I had ever recognized instantly as queer. His personality had the flair, style, and pizazz associated with Northeast, big-city, theatre-type folks. He filled a room on entry, even without saying a word—much like a grand lady of Hollywood or the stage. The store itself served as an outlet for his passions around design and decoration and he had a same-sex life partner about whom he loved to tell stories and who would occasionally visit. The stories were nothing crude or risqué, just simple normal people together tales. These everyday life insights opened a possibility to me I had never before considered. He never pushed the gay issue with me, and he never tried to drag me unwillingly out of any comfort zone. There was never even a pointed question about my sexuality or what I thought it might be. Because of the polite, respectful nature of our conversations and his good-natured, positive example of what life was like for him as a gay man, the camera store evolved into a safe space to explore in my mind the reality of my identity. I edged closer to a degree of acknowledgment and acceptance instead of outright terror about who I was in the world.

I even managed an awkward intimate encounter with someone I met at another of my jobs, serving as the weekend manager of the Ronald McDonald House adjacent to Tampa General Hospital. That midnight experience of about fifteen awkward minutes validated every inner suspicion about my sexual identity but also scared the shit out of me. Setting the stage for future events, he was slightly younger, Latino, and from someplace distant so there was little chance of anything else happening. At that moment, and for the next four years, I would enact a twisted policy of my own about my orientation—it would become not only "don't ask" but "don't do" as well.

Thankfully, I had retained my interest in the fire service and radios and managed to start a fire buff's organization during my time in Florida. Our club would end up with about twenty members consisting of dispatchers, retired firefighters, volunteer firefighters, and other enthusiasts. Again, a hobby served to occupy time that most others would use for dating. Hanging out with people talking about the fire service filled a void I might have otherwise used to explore my newly developing identity. But given I was in the South, the views of my conservative parents, and a mysterious tether back to a religious identity I had abandoned at thirteen, I just did not see living into my truth as an option. Instead of dating, I spent more and more time working and hanging out with friends.

One new friend was a supervisor in the Tampa Fire Communications Office, and I would make a point to visit him at the center regularly. This was my first experience spending serious time in a large city's fire dispatch office. Watching the small group of professionals process and dispatch alarms was fascinating, especially during major fires. They dispatched units, managed resources, yelled at each other across the floor, and operated as an incredible single unit devoted to one highly important mission even in the midst of a high-stress environment.

The building and technology were antiquated at best, but the people who worked there did their jobs with a passionate commitment that was always a delight to watch. I enjoyed every minute and would even bring them food on hectic nights, fetching pizzas for them from the Domino's down the street.

In 1994, my friend, who had previously lived in Jamaica, Queens and served as an auxiliary firefighter in the FDNY, invited me on a quick road trip to New York City. After a tortuous drive straight through from Tampa to the borough of Queens, we slept for a while and then explored the city and visited his friends and family.

Seeing New York for the first time in person was not what I expected. We did not venture into Manhattan, staying in Brooklyn and Queens due to our limited time, and the skyline of Manhattan—the Twin Towers, The Empire State Building, and all the symbolism remained distant visions. Instead, I was treated to "real" New York. Houses not unlike those in older parts of Columbus, but more densely packed, a significantly more diverse population of people than I had ever seen, plus double parking, and crazy traffic. We connected with a few of his friends who worked in the fire department. They were gruff and not the warmest of people, but overall, the experience left me intrigued but not completely changed. I was left wanting more and definitely not turned off of New York in any way. I had a slightly better reaction to my first quick stop at an FDNY Central Office (or dispatch center). It was only a few moments, but I still remember the archaic screens, the dispatchers smoking on the floor and the feeling that it was more an old school bar atmosphere than a center for critical communications. Nonetheless, it felt like someplace I wanted to spend more time. I had no idea, of course, just how much my future would involve that very building.

On the second night, we went to "ride" with one of the five heavy rescue companies tasked with responding to the most serious incidents and fires in New York. We were the guests of Rescue Company Four, quartered in a seventy-five-year-old firehouse on Queens Boulevard near the Brooklyn Queens Expressway and would spend the night tour with them. This meant spending about fourteen hours in the firehouse and experiencing every aspect of a typical fire department shift. This has been a time-honored tradition in the fire service, especially in larger and busier departments for as long as there have been fire departments. Riders will spend time for a number of reasons—to learn about other departments, to experience a family member's job, to see different tactics, or to get a small taste of what it's like to be a part of the experience that is FDNY.

Spending the shift in the firehouse was like something out of a dream. I will never forget the residual smell of smoke from turnout gear and equipment that had been to countless fires blended with the fuel for power tools and the food being cooked in the kitchen. The hazy echoes of responses in the days of horse-drawn fire apparatus that filled the firehouse. It had a language all of its own that you felt when you walked in the door. They were welcoming and kind to guests, except when my snoring woke someone up that night. The meal was an inspiring display of culinary skill, and the stories and conversations that evening made up a world that instantly drew me into it.

In a remarkable feat of irony, one thing we did not do was ride to any "runs." Our arrival, as so often happens when riders used to be able to do such things, was on an astonishingly quiet shift. Instead of riders, we became "sitters." Nevertheless, I could not wait to go back and do it again. I would be able to recreate the experience with more substantial and exciting results a few years later. As it was, our trip ended, and we made our way back. Somewhere along the equally tortuous drive back to Florida, I knew that I had to get out of Florida. I knew it was the worst possible fit and that my path would eventually take me to New York City. I had no idea how, but I knew. What I did not see yet was the FDNY as my full career path. Oddly, the experience of visiting FDNY and spending time in New York even for only a couple of days, did not deter my original vision of being an international diplomat or other government role, just confirmed that the Fire Department was one of the things I would love about the city I wanted to live in.

6 | THE FIRE DEPARTMENT JOURNEY BEGINS

I decided the first step would be moving back to Ohio, which I did just before Christmas in 1994. Reconnecting with friends I had left behind during my palm tree sojourn, I was happy to hear a part-time fire dispatching job was available at my hometown fire department. I applied around Christmas and was hired after several interviews, starting in early February 1995. The training was a series of shifts sitting with one of the three full-time dispatchers. There was no formal curriculum, just learning through observation and practice. I was fortunate to answer a call for a working fire within my first week or two. The caller was trying to report what was happening, but the line went dead. Thankfully, we already had the address and had heard the word *fire*. My trainer sardonically assured me the fire companies would arrive to find a working fire because the line went dead after being burned through. His intuition proved correct, and my career as a dispatcher was off and running.

There was never any additional formalized training during my five-plus years there. It was indeed a learn-as-you-go kind of place. The arrangement was typical. The dispatch office was the front room of the fire station, and we served as greeters and dispatchers. We also interacted extensively with the firefighters and were always invited to eat meals with them. I would hang out at the firehouse sometimes when I was off and was able to ride with them to incidents. This helped me increase not just my knowledge about the job but also my bonds with the people I worked with. For the almost frighteningly serious responsibility, I was compensated $5.84 per hour. I would work weekend shifts at the fire department in addition to going to school and working at a camera shop, which helped advance my interest in photography with the technical support and employee discounts.

It was a crazy busy time, being reacclimated to life in Ohio, working multiple jobs, and living at home. It was also a time of denial. I assumed that my parents would never be supportive or accepting of my sexual orientation. I also thought that working in the fire department, even as a dispatcher, would not be the most positive environment for me to show who I really was. Further, I did not see my old friend group of fire department enthusiasts, the old straight white guys, as well as the new friends I would make in the firehouse as potential allies around "non-traditional" sexual orientation.

As a result, I continued my devil's bargain and convinced myself that I would just ignore my sexuality until some later date when it would all work itself out. Writing those words all these years later makes me smile at how naive this plan was. More so, it was also terribly harmful. It never occurred to me to talk to someone like a therapist or even consider talking to my family about it. It was a burden I decided to swallow whole and address on my own.

Unsurprisingly, by working in the firehouse, I started developing even more friendships with people associated with the fire department. These were all straight, younger guys in their twenties who had two primary hobbies—drinking and girls. It was the closest thing I would ever know to being a fraternity member. I enjoyed the company and the conversation. I fell right into this group of great friends and colleagues while balancing the fear that, at some point, they would come to know who I really was, and then it would be over.

On my return to college at the Ohio State University, I found myself on suddenly shaky ground. Originally, I had initially planned to major in

Spanish and international relations at South Florida, but that plan had failed. Now, after my return to Ohio, I had no idea what I really wanted to do with my education. I also felt the burden of feeling like the move had been a failure. And I had no real idea of what my long-term career might be. And there were answers about my sexual orientation, but it felt like that part of my life would forever have to be denied and ignored. When that situation collided with the consistent pressure from parents who had expected me to have had it all figured out, I started to crack. Early on in my return to Ohio State, in the last third of the quarter, I just stopped going to class. I can't share what I did instead. It was sort of a month or two long breakdown and collapse. I think it was a great deal of drinking with newfound friends and working, but the strain, stress, and fear had found their release in the explosion of my academic career. I did not reach out to any counselor or advisor at school to share my frustration. I did not have an honest and upfront conversation with a trusted friend. I just sucked it up and kept about my business, except, of course, for the part about school. The end result was four Fs, a couple of very confused professors who tried to reach out but who I pushed away, and me having even less of an idea about where I was supposed to go in the world and who I was supposed to be.

The confusion continued for the rest of 1995 and included a very short stint at a full-time police and fire dispatcher job and an effort to attend the local community college on my academic probation induced break from Ohio State. In every way, those experiences felt even worse than being at Ohio State and only served to make my life more confusing. Within about an hour of my first shift with the suburban police 911 center in a very wealthy suburb near Columbus, I knew that I had again made a big mistake. It was the same feeling I had felt in Florida walking onto the campus of my backup choice university. I felt the same way sitting in a 100-level class at community college. It wasn't that I was any better or that I was above where I was, but it was like wearing ill-fitting clothes. They were suitable for someone else but not right for me. It was a moment of looking around and realizing that not only that choice had been a mistake. Almost everything I had decided to do since my senior year of high school was questionable in motive because it involved my attempts to navigate a world where I did not feel at place, at peace, or myself.

One thing I did know was that I wanted to be back at Ohio State. That felt right, to the point I regretted not just going there straight out of high school. Within a week of the full-time dispatch job starting, I had applied for reinstatement at Ohio State, been conditionally accepted, and started thinking about where I ultimately wanted to live. That decision was made easier by a trip I had made a few months before: my first to New York City where I was not the ride-along person but someone on a mission to figure out everything I could about New York City and strategize how I could eventually live there.

That trip had been in June of 1995, and I was accompanied by one of my new friends from the fire department where I worked. It had been arranged by someone I had found in a guidebook list of fire department enthusiasts from around the world, organized by name, location, types of interests, and other factors. My newly found friend was an FDNY dispatcher who had moved to New York City from New England. We quickly developed a long-distance, fire service enthusiast and dispatcher-based friendship. Beyond being a dispatcher, he was an author of history books about the FDNY making him an expert on the history of not just the department but also the firehouses as well and the individual fire companies. He offered to help set up FDNY history tours for me if I visited New York. An offer I very quickly accepted.

It was mid-June 1995 when I made the first nine-hour road trip from Columbus to New York City. The four-day trip far exceeded expectations. From visiting my new friend at the Brooklyn Central (Dispatch) Office (which would become my first FDNY dispatch assignment in 2000) to riding along at firehouses all over the city and exploring the tourist sites, it was a perfect adventure. One place high on our list to visit was the World

Trade Center. All of New York City, the harbor, and northern New Jersey were visible from the rooftop viewing area, even on that grey foggy day. It was a perfect view to take it all in and consider the size and scale of that expansive metropolis. Of course, we had no idea what would come, and that it would be the first and last time I would stand on that deck. That moment and that trip settled the big question of where I was going to end up, even if it did not reveal the process that would make it happen. I was going to move to New York City.

FDNY had a mystique that had captivated the American fire service for decades. It still does to this day, a presence that owes some of its significance to the events surrounding September 11, 2001. Even before then, thanks to the heroic efforts of many FDNY members at countless fires and rescues, quite a few of which were covered on national TV news, FDNY was so much more than a fire department. Its dispatchers were legendary as well, at least in the circles where that was possible. I had listened to audio tapes of their radio traffic and seen videos shared in the fire buff community of their incredible ability to manage units and incidents during incredibly busy periods, learned about their position as the ringmaster of all that was going on the in the fire department, and seen them as professional role-models even before I became a dispatcher myself. Above the door in the former Bronx Central Office was a sign that read, "Through these doors walk the best damn dispatchers in the world." Hyperbole, perhaps, but the words rang true in that first big trip to New York City in 1995. It was the greatest city, the greatest fire department, and someplace I wanted to be.

Over the next few years, I would make the trip to New York City at least twice a year, mostly driving and occasionally flying. Most of the time, I took different fire department buddies, for whom the chance to visit the FDNY was like going to Universal Studios, Disney World, and every other amusement park rolled into one. My friends were all too happy to go along on the trip, and sharing the experience with others was fun. One downside, however, was that I never got to explore a side of New York that may have helped me figure out who I was outside of the fire service. There were no gay bar or club adventures where I tested my increasing self-awareness and my simultaneous increasing self-rejection and denial. I took my closet with me when I visited New York. It was as though each side of me lived unconnected to the other, and I was going to make a lifetime commitment to maintaining that condition.

On my return to Ohio State, I decided that I would try an experiment of sorts to figure out my future educational path. I read the entire course catalog. I picked out the top four courses that interested me and that I thought might serve as guideposts to future careers. Aviation, Philosophy, English, and Urban Geography were those selections. I did very well in all of them, shaken by my previous experiences to the point of focus. The Urban Geography course, in particular, stirred my soul. It focused on how communities organize and develop, how to make them more livable, and how they are governed. It was fascinating, authentic, and related to my long-held passion for cities and communities.

I felt like my nine-year-old self, walking around downtown Columbus on summer days while my dad was working in his office at the federal building. The spark was fired, and, within weeks, I declared a major in Geography, Urban and Regional Studies, with a minor in History. I had found my educational calling and would never look back. My grades would never again crater at Ohio State. The foundation of Urban Geography did not just provide me with a degree, but also validated some of the lessons I would learn over the next twenty-five years of my professional career. The most important things that communities can offer are opportunities and safety. This includes the opportunity to raise a family, build friendships, and create the types of connections that help us make our way through our ordinary daily lives and the most stressful of times.

Similarly, at their best, communities offer the security for each member of the community to be their authentic selves, free from harm or threat. The most effective organizations or teams also reflect these realities as well as the negative results when people do not feel safe or secure. It is only when people feel that sense of security and are part of something bigger than themselves that towns, cities, teams, or our entire world can move forward. One of the greatest gifts that a fire department provides its members, when it is an effective organization, is a culture of trust and respect that supports feelings of security and belonging. This is why, although I was happy to be a part of something helpful overall, I was still terrified of upending my sense of belonging by exploring or admitting who I was.

The dark side of communities is their potential lack of tolerance for people who do not fit the mold, who can be perceived as threatening the cohesiveness of the group. These dynamics have only become more visible in our modern time of social media and algorithms, where groups can play up the "threat of the outsider on our cohesive group" without people even realizing it. Thankfully, social media was only in its infancy when I came out. I was more inspired by the security of belonging to my fire service community than I was scared of blowing it up. In truth, the increasing feeling of belonging in my academic self also freed me up to explore the rest of me and begin the process of coming out.

7 | COMING OUT

There are so many myths and misunderstandings around the topic of coming out. Fortunately, over the last couple of decades, the process has become more accessible for many people. It also appears that the average age at which people decide to come out has been trending downward, at least giving the impression that it is an easier and more accepted event than in the past. The polls on societal endorsement have shown support for same-sex marriage at its highest numbers ever, and the world just "feels" like a more tolerant place than it was. However, recent battles against the evils of drag queens and pride parades and policy votes by major religious organizations may indicate some backsliding. That is unfortunate, sad, and in some ways dangerous. Thankfully, we are still better off than we were twenty-five years ago with room to grow as a society, which, of course, we must do.

The reality is that coming out is not done based on a poll, and it is not, at first, a community experience. It is entirely and wholly personal. The first and last person with whom you make peace about who you are is, in fact, you. The community around you can help make that process easier, or it can make it harder, as with family, friends, and society in general. However, it starts and ends with the person who looks back at you from the mirror when you accept who you have been made to be and tell your truth out loud, perhaps for the first time.

The second common misunderstanding is that a person only comes out once. It is as though there is one particular day, like a birthday, where there is a clear before and a clear after, and nothing is the same again now that this one specific issue is put to bed forever and ever. Nothing could be further from the truth. Not only are we as human beings more complex than that, but everyone interacts at differing levels with different members of their communities. This is especially true when it comes to personal or private bits of information. You may not want to share a terrible medical diagnosis with everyone you work with, but it would feel impossible not to share it with your work bestie. Likewise, you may not tell your kids right away about losing a job, especially if that happens right before Christmas and you want to protect them from the stress, anguish, and trauma they might feel.

In a nation where you can still be fired in many states for being gay, and where political and legal battles continue to this day regarding LGBTQ+IA rights, it can be a matter of safety and security to not be your authentic self with everyone all at once. When you are part of a community where attitudes and even policies are less than affirming, such as a church or fire department, it can be an essential task, even in the present day, to weigh the risks versus the rewards of coming out. Some more militant members of the LGBTQ+IA community may dismiss this as an old-fashioned and unrealistic fear in the era of social media and the shaming of organizations that are intolerant. However, the reality of where the next paycheck will come from if you are fired, or of being ostracized from a community that is important to you, or any other number of possible side effects, is real and terrifying. They were even more so when, in 1997, I decided to begin the process of coming out not just in my personal life but ultimately in my professional life as well.

By that point, the burden of living two lives had become too much to bear. I had been back at Ohio State for two years and had fallen in love with my degree program. I was in my second year of working as a fire dispatcher and had fallen equally in love with my job and what it entailed. It felt like most of me was traveling on the right track. I had also started visiting New York regularly, which helped me develop a North Star. I knew that was where I wanted to end up, and the only part I had to figure out was the process of making it happen. However much was going right, I was still holding back the truth about myself. I was approaching twenty-three years old, and life as some sort of celibate, closeted, ex-Christian was less appealing by the day. This was also the time of increasing public acceptance around the issue. Ellen DeGeneres's coming out and the eventual arrival of *Will and Grace* were noteworthy examples. For me, it was simpler than that. I understood that I just could not go on ignoring who I was.

The fear of being ostracized by my friends or family was real. Ultimately, I decided that if my friends were my friends, they would accept me no matter what. If they scattered because of this news, they were never my friends anyway. The irony was that the same security I felt in being a part of a school and a fire department that felt like home meant I felt strong enough for at least one of those things to go away if the reaction were negative.

I did not, however, have the same degree of self-assuredness about the potential reaction of my family. Growing up with Baptist parents, there was minimal discussion of sex in the home at all. I only recall a few vague comments about gay people, and those were probably directed at Elton John and likely not positive. Generally, the topic was ignored, although by the time I was in my early twenties I had never brought home a girl in any form to meet the family. They had to have sensed that something was up, even if they never addressed it to me directly.

Circumstances with my family changed in 1998 when my dad retired from his job with the state of Ohio. As a result, one of my mom's dreams came true. She, my dad, and my sister decided to move to Florida. As happy as I was for my mom that she would be able to move within a few miles of her beloved jetty, I have to confess I was even happier to know that with their distance would come my freedom. It also meant I would be homeless as soon as they moved, so I had a personal and practical interest in finding somewhere to live. With gleeful anticipation, I began scouring the newspapers for apartment listings. I searched for just the right place to not only start my own life in Columbus, but also to start living into who I was. As a lover of geography and maps, it should come as no surprise that I recognized the power of place to support a transformation. I was fully aware that no suburban garden apartment was going to meet my needs. This was how I found my way to a tiny listing in the newspaper classifieds for the Townley Court Apartments on Town Street in downtown Columbus.

8 | MIRACLE ON TOWN STREET

My visit to the rental office to inquire about the apartment I had seen in the advertisement was the stuff of legends. The manager was straight out of *Golden Girls* central casting, with a splash of *Tales of the City* thrown in for good measure. Armistead Maupin would have been immensely proud. She scanned me up and down in the office lobby and said almost nothing from behind her chain-hooked glasses until the assessment was complete. She then decreed, "Okay, let me take you to where you are going to live." There would be paperwork later, but at that moment, I knew my world had changed for the better and that I was standing on the edge of something entirely new and necessary. With that, we walked across the street to the back building of the complex and the top-floor corner studio apartment where I would do so much of my growing up over the next two years.

Growing up primarily meant coming out and, along the way, graduating from Ohio State University as well as getting ready to move to New York City. Within a day or two of moving in, I made new friends, including a gay uncle of sorts who guessed my intentions with the move right away and became my tour guide to a side of Columbus I had never before experienced. Armed with that essential knowledge of the bars to go to, the people to avoid and the general lay of the land, I was able to explore and embrace my new home. Along the way, I started the process of coming out to friends. Nearly every conversation occurred on the barstools at the legendary Thurman Café in Columbus. I would invite my friend to dinner. We would eat. I would then clear my throat, take an empowering long sip of beer, and summon the nerve to say, "I have something I need to tell you." Without fail, each of my friends would look at me and say, "If you are going to tell me you are gay, don't bother. I know already, and it's not a problem." My friends not only did not reject me, but they offered something even better: acceptance. Armed with that empowering sense of place, I made my way out into the world and turned my attention to the place of my employment and my family.

At the firehouse, where I was working thirty hours a week, I had expanded my role to include training new hires and supporting other agencies seeking to provide training or improve operations. I enjoyed fire dispatching; it was like a three-dimensional chess game where you never knew how all the pieces would move. Thankfully, my department was not terribly busy, so the slow times were perfect for doing schoolwork or engaging in long conversations with the firefighters and officers working at the station. One of my coworkers, in the middle of one of those slow nights and during an extensive group discussion about history, politics, religion, or some other major topic, offered an only slightly coded suggestion that I should consider coming out. It took me back a bit, as I had not been sure he or anyone else in the firehouse knew. It was clear he did, and I had to process for a while whether or not I was ready to take that step.

There were no out gay men that I knew of in the fire service of central Ohio, and this would be a huge step. I considered it and ultimately decided on the easiest path forward. I ensured that the biggest gossip in the firehouse found out about it. There is something to be said for the indirect method. The beauty of it was that the vast majority of people I worked with gave me a hug or a handshake. They said they loved me and would defend me against anyone who ever messed with me. The exact language was a bit tougher than that; after all, it was the firefighters I was talking to. Yes, there were challenges with a couple of people, but that was to be expected. We ended up having a conversation around the chief's conference table that was moderated by a mutual friend. It was not mandated or because of an HR complaint but because I wanted to give them the opportunity to talk to me about their concerns. This was as new to them as it was to me. I was, in fact, the very first gay person they had ever known. I would like to say that everything was perfect from that moment forward and that they became my biggest supporters, but that would not be accurate or realistic. They were professional and distant for the rest of my time there, which was okay. They were not harmful or rude, just distant. Not everyone needs to be your best friend, even in a firehouse.

What was far better than okay would occur in June of 1999, a year before my move to New York, when I held a "coming out at the firehouse/graduating from Ohio State" party at my favorite gay bar/restaurant in Columbus. Over forty of my coworkers and friends showed up, sang along with the singer I hired for the event, and spent hours shooting pool with the "neighborhood gays" in the bar next door. As my fire chief bought people shots of Patron tequila and sang along with the show tunes he knew, it was apparent that I had made the correct decision in terms of moving where I did, coming out when I did, and trusting the people I worked with to know the real me. Although terrifying at times, I would not have come out any other way. The miraculous and inspiring way that the fire service, Ohio State, and my little corner of Gay Columbus embraced me only further inspired me to do big things and dream bigger dreams. What all of them at the party knew about and had helped to inspire was a trip I had made two months before in April of 1999. It was then that I sat for the New York City Civil Service Exam for Fire Alarm Dispatcher.

9 | THE TEST

In visiting the city, conversing with new friends there, and reflecting on where I wanted to be in my life, it was obvious that New York City was the place. It was so obvious I would occasionally get frustrated with myself because I had not thought of it sooner. Perhaps I could have avoided that expensive detour to Florida. Well, things happen when they are supposed to, and now my plan was in place. I would wait for the test results, and if I did well enough to get hired on at the FDNY, I would move there, work for a few years as a dispatcher while going to school for my master's degree and then go find my "real" career in government or at the United Nations.

Any doubt about that plan was eradicated on that visit to New York when I took the civil service exam in April of 1999. That was a trip I made solo. I flew from Columbus to LaGuardia Airport and planned a four-night stay. I had to take the civil service exam at John Jay High School in the Richmond Hill Section of Queens on a Saturday morning. The rest of the time, I wanted to finally explore New York City as an out gay man. Free of straight friends along for the FDNY experience, I had just enough awareness of the geography of New York City to know where to go, or at least a reasonably good idea. I booked a hotel near Herald Square, putting me in the middle of Manhattan. It was just a few blocks from the prime "gayborhoods" of Chelsea and the West Village. I was also within walking distance of many tourist spots and not even that far from Central Park.

Upon checking into the stereotypically tiny hotel room with just enough room for a bed and the door to open, I left the hotel to find the home of the LGBTQ Community Center. It had moved to a temporary home on the edge of the West Village, near West 14th Street. I must have looked like a kid at Disney World when I walked in and asked what information the volunteer at the desk might have to help a recently out gay guy from Ohio in the process of getting ready to move to New York City. Thank God the girl at the desk was kind and supportive. We talked for nearly an hour about what it was like to live in New York. She, too, had been a transplant. In time, I would realize that almost everyone I would ever meet in Manhattan would be some sort of transplant. Even if they had moved there from an outer borough of the city, upstate, or Long Island, they had still moved with the sincere intention of flipping the script of their lives. They would have remained where they were if they had wanted the status quo, where it was easy to avoid the harsh realities that eventually settle in after following your dream to move to the big city. The front desk person directed me to a stack of guides and magazines. She suggested I circle a few bars in the listing that I might like to visit and plan my evenings in Manhattan. I took my homework instruction eagerly, thanked her profusely for her time, and found someplace for dinner in Chelsea.

I was exhausted, so I went back to the hotel, sat up in bed, and began to read the descriptions of the various bars and dance clubs in Manhattan. There were more than I could have imagined—page upon page of listings. It was like the restaurant listings back in Columbus, with something for every palate and something for every taste. I saw several that really interested me. One in particular stood out. In the paragraph, under the essential details like its address and what subway lines were closest, the words sounded like those of my favorite haunts back in Columbus: friendly, neighborhood bar loved by locals and visitors alike. It was called The Cubbyhole. I made sure to put extra circles around that listing.

The next evening, after hours of exploring Manhattan and enjoying a sidewalk café dinner, I made my way to The Cubbyhole, one of the smallest bars I have ever encountered anywhere. It was crowded. I was understandably nervous. It felt like walking into a new church where you did not know a soul. I navigated through the tightly packed crowd and was exultant to see an empty bar stool. I noticed it was covered, as were all the bar stools, with Looney Tunes cartoon characters. As I sat down, I realized that plastic characters were hanging from every inch of the ceiling—like what you would find in a party store. They were mostly multi-colored fish.

Then, I had a feeling in the pit of my stomach that something was off. I looked around over both shoulders and scanned the crowd I had just passed through, including the bartender and the other patrons perched on the bar stools. As it turned out, I was the only boy in the bar. I had apparently missed one small detail, reflected by a logo at the top of the magazine listing. This was a lesbian bar, and not just any lesbian bar but one of the most famous in the city of New York. Just then a very gruff voice came from my right. I braced myself for what I was sure would be a scolding. "You can sit there, but only 'cause you are kinda cute." I couldn't help but roar with laughter and then she did, too. I replied that her introduction was so funny I had to buy her a Corona. Her response was, "Enough with that shit; I'm buying you a shot of tequila." And that is how my first big gay night in New York City really got started.

We talked at the bar and with those around us for hours. It must have been three or four hours later when she shared she was getting hungry and asked if I wanted to grab food. With that, we started off into the Village night for a Chinese restaurant. In the middle of West Fourth Street, with a light rain now falling, she stopped, turned back to me, grabbed my shoulders, and said, "You know what I am going to do for you? What I wish someone would have done for me!" I did not have the chance to get out a snide joke about the girls who had tried to convert me during my freshman year of college. Before I could say anything, she said, "Guided tour, gay New York, tonight, on me."

So began one of the best random-stranger-in-big-city adventures I would ever experience. The Chinese food was first, then a few more lesbian bars. Then there were some mixed bars and then a few focused more on guys. At 3:00 in the morning, she left me at the front door of a gay New York City institution, just off Sheridan Square: The Monster. "You will find a boy here to get you home," she said. "My work here is done." With that and a quick exchange of email addresses my Mary Poppins, Dolly Parton, and Good Witch Glinda all rolled into one vanished into the night. Standing on that street corner, just feet away from where the Stonewall Riots happened in 1969, ushering in a new level of the gay rights movement, feeling the history and possibility around me, I could have levitated all the way back to Ohio—if I had wanted to go back there at all. I knew I was home and that things would not be right until this place was my official home. I had been granted an amazing gift: the door to a new world had been opened. It was going to be mine. Sadly, I would never reconnect with my new friend; I don't think it was the kind of friendship that was long-term anyway. It was a circumstantial connection, brought to fruition by a series of random events that lose something if you try to fully understand the circumstances that created them, losing even more if we try to replicate them.

I went into The Monster. I wandered around for a bit, had a drink, talked to a couple of people, and somehow made my way back to my hotel. Twenty-eight hours later, I would be standing in a line of about six hundred fifty people waiting to enter a classic New York City high school to take a civil service exam for the job I hoped would reopen that door to this fantastic new world. The test was a combination of audio scenarios played over the high school's speaker system and a written exam. I will confess it felt easy then, but I was nervous. There was so much riding on what I was doing—so much expectation at this moment. It would take a long time to get the results—over a year—and by then, I would be living in New York City.

The most challenging part of the expected job was the salary of FDNY fire dispatchers and the reality that more than $27,865.00 annually would be needed to support a life in New York without food stamps or roommates. In time, the plan was developed to get a couple of my Columbus friends to move to New York with me. The idea was born while travelling back to Columbus in April of 1999 and was a done deal in early 2000. There were several road trips to New York with my potential roommates to check out neighborhoods and figure out where we wanted to live. My employment with FDNY would require me to live within the city limits, as residency in the city was a requirement. My familiarity with Brooklyn and Staten Island meant those boroughs were our early focus. The price of Manhattan apartments meant those were out of reach.

The search for an apartment for us to share took us to dozens of potential spaces. Some were okay; some were terrible. From a three-bedroom apartment in Staten Island that reeked of curry, to Park Slope Brooklyn where the price alone ended even the thought of looking, the apartment hunt was in many ways one of the most stressful aspects of trying to live in New York City. Our ultimate decision to use a broker whose ad we saw in the paper would save us time but not save us money.

By May of 2000, thanks to that broker, we had found an apartment, put down the extreme initial fees of first and last month's rent and one month's security deposit, and had our move date picked out. We would move the fourth weekend of June, in the year 2000, to Bay Ridge, a neighborhood on the southwest corner of Brooklyn, near the Verrazano Bridge and easily connected to the rest of the city by subway and bus. The three of us would be roommates, splitting the very expensive apartment, and we would build our new lives in New York City. Everything was going to work out magically—until it didn't.

10 | THE PLAN

The connections the three of us had before moving to New York were likely not the best foundations. We were really acquaintances sharing a situation more deserving of a Herman Melville novel than a spinoff of the TV series *Friends*. One friend was a neighbor I had gotten to know in the Columbus gay scene. Although he was undoubtedly physically attractive, his more important qualities were a bubbly, outgoing personality and an infectious magnetism that made him someone I enjoyed being around. He also had his demons that I would only come to fully appreciate a few years later. It was likely because of those combined qualities that I also saw him as someone who needed a friend and some stability. I even thought that the move to New York might provide him with a much-needed fresh start where he could reinvent himself and escape at least some of the drama that always seemed to be chasing him. Together, these were just the kind of services a Virgo with a rescue complex like me was all too happy to provide.

When the plans for the New York move were hatched, he was pretty excited to join the effort, although I failed to fully understand how much adding people to teams could impact the other team members. The other group member was a neighbor friend who lived in my apartment building, one floor below. He was the best straight friend a newly out gay guy could ask for and was, in fact, the very first person I ever told I was gay. That fact permanently infuriated my "big gay uncle" neighbor, who was offended beyond measure he had not been the first to officially know, even though he had, of course, unofficially suspected. My trusted straight friend would go with me to any bar, so long as no gay folks tried to touch him. He could sit for hours and just watch the show, being my wingman of sorts. He rarely looked for any of his own among the straight girls who would sometimes be in attendance. They might be on their own quests for entertainment, tag-a-longs for their gay friends or brothers or wanting to go out and have a good time without worrying about a bunch of leering guys giving them a hard time. My buddy would offer me advice and support when the many romantic campaigns I launched in my early years of the bar scene so often crashed down, like Snoopy versus the Red Baron. Luckily, we survived that era, and along the way, I was fortunate to make many new friends who would shepherd me into the new life I was living, and the move that I had long suspected I had to make.

Sadly, my straight friend did not like the other member of the team moving to the city. On the night of our going away party, he announced to me that he was no longer willing or able to move, several thousand dollars in deposits, signed rental agreements, and a crowded bar full of people waiting to wish us well notwithstanding. He shared this news as we were getting ready to head to the party from our apartment building. Practically, this last-minute decision blew up the business plan for our move. The apartment was not workable with just two roommates. There was now no way we could afford to go. My New York dream evaporated into the futon I was sitting on when he told me. I was consumed by sadness, anger, and disappointment in waves that alternated between pushing me toward the floor of my apartment to wail, wanting to beat the shit out of my friend, and wanting to find a solution—any solution—to help make this plan still work and keep my dream of moving to New York City alive.

A few months before this shattering night, a new person had started hanging out in the neighborhood at the same bars and restaurants I frequented. He was an easy person to talk to and, owing to his West Virginia roots, pleasant enough in a superficial kind of way. He had shared his own dreams of moving to New York City with me a few times over the previous month. Shortly after arriving at our party and still processing my friend's devastating revelation, I saw this new friend near the bar. When I saw him, the idea occurred to me instantly. Why not him? The portion of my dream clinging to any possibility of survival said to him, "So—want to move to New York?" His smile in response to the question gave me his answer immediately, long before he said anything or discussed any details. He only asked if I was serious. I said yes, and then we solved our dilemma. The dream had survived, New York City was back on, and I was willing to speak to my friend again—although I still wanted to strangle him for putting me through all of that.

Even by the standards of people who party with seriousness, the party was epic. All three of us who had initially been moving to New York had large groups of friends and connections. There were people from the fire department, coworkers of both friends, and Ohio State University folks. A cornucopia of people was there to send us off, even though the actual departure date was not for three weeks. Several group members stayed to tell stories, laugh, and drink until closing, all of us sharing in the glow and joy of people heading out to follow a dream. It was a beautiful and powerful event, but also bittersweet. Here we were, moving away from all this. We were forsaking, in a way, a home each of us had created to hopefully find, build, and succeed in a new one. As heartwarming as it was to share that experience and its possibilities, it was also sad to acknowledge what we were leaving behind and might not find again, even if we were to return. No one else knew about the change in plans that had nearly upended the entire process. No one else really knew the person who would now be joining us, and no one had any idea, especially me, of the horror that would happen only a few hours later.

11 | SURVIVAL

The party went very late, right up to the Columbus bar closing time of 2:30 a.m. My initial future roommate, who was sleeping on my couch for the last few days in Columbus to save money, found a more affectionate crash pad for the after party in the form of a person he had long tried to hook-up with, so I was initially going to have the apartment to myself that evening. Hearing this, the new addition to the moving adventure came back to my apartment with me so we could talk about the plans. He then asked if he could crash at my place and head home in the morning because he had a bit too much to drink. "Yes, of course," I said without any hesitation. After all, if I couldn't trust this guy to sleep on my couch, how could I trust him to move to New York with me?

It must have been around 3:30 a.m. when I passed out. The apartment I had been introduced to on that beautiful day two years before was a large studio with a sleeping area, a living area, a kitchen and dining room, and a walk-in closet. It was on the third floor of a building that did not feel like it belonged in Columbus, Ohio, but rather in Boston or Chicago. Sitting alongside a cobbled street with trees meeting above the streets to form a canopy, its history and the essence of all the lives lived there before were palpable. The apartment was small and cheap (only $335 a month in rent), but it was one of the most authentic homes I would ever know. I had fallen in love with the view of the downtown skyline and the easy walk to a neighborhood bar that catered to the gay communities of downtown and

Old Towne East. It was only a ten-minute drive to the campus of Ohio State and about a fifteen-minute drive to the firehouse where I worked as a dispatcher. It was at the epicenter of everything I did and could not have been more perfect for those last two years in Columbus. The bar, where I had hung out with my new friend and where he would ultimately get a job as a waiter, was my other home for four or five nights a week. It served as the bridge between a straight suburban childhood and the urban not so straight me I thought I was becoming, but in reality, I already was.

It was in this apartment, my safe space, my home in which I grew more than anywhere else I have ever lived, that I woke a few hours after falling asleep to an experience I could not fully understand even as it was happening.

It was disorienting and weird and, at first, more frustrating than terrifying. I woke up with the realization that I was being held down, that someone was on top of me and slowly, very slowly, I began to realize I needed to resist. It took a minute to recognize who I was fighting against, where I had been held, and what was actually happening. I fought, I am pretty sure I kicked, and maybe even bit, too, and then it ended. In the grand scheme of things, it felt then as it does now: like a moment in the looking glass, where down was up and up was down. I realized that I was being attacked. Someone was trying "to have their way with me." I also felt utterly removed from the situation, as though I was watching it from a distance. My fight was real enough, though, and it ended within a moment or two. I had been successful, I thought, but in my disconnected state, under the influence of what I assumed was alcohol, I did not fully realize what had happened.

Instead, I fell back asleep for a few hours. A few hours later, I remember waking and feeling like everything was off-center. It was as if a giant earthquake had occurred, but only to me. I felt terribly sick in my gut, as though I had overeaten horrible food and went immediately to bed. I wanted to throw up but could not find the energy at first to make it to the bathroom. I vaguely remembered the sensations from the night before, the struggle, the wrestling, and some vague memories of words spoken, but I dismissed them as a dream, something not real, something imagined.

Regaining just enough sense of where I was, I put my feet on the floor beside my bed. It was early—far earlier than it should have been the morning after such a fantastic party. I noticed my new potential roommate was awake, too. I managed to drag myself to the bathroom. Standing in the black and white tiled room, with a bit of space from my guest, I started to remember a little more about the dreams. I increasingly knew that something horrible had happened. I also knew more than anything that I wanted this person out of my apartment. I knew that I was not in a safe space with him there. I did the only thing I could think of doing to get him out and offered to drive him home.

I remember how quiet he was. He had next to no words when I made the offer to drive him home, when he accepted, and when I quickly got ready to leave. He said almost nothing; he just sat on the couch waiting to go. It was then, starting to leave the apartment, that I remember looking down at my arms and seeing marks and the start of bruising. I knew then, sort of, what had happened. I was still mainly in a fog, but a quick, ice-cold bath of feeling poured over me at that moment, offering a glimpse of what had occurred several hours before. It still did not feel totally real. What was real, totally and completely, was the sensation of cold. It lasted for the duration of the short drive to his nearby apartment. Why I did not just make him walk, I will never know. Thankfully, it was only five minutes, then he was gone. I knew at the moment he got out of the car that I was safer than I had been than with him in it. I drove back to my apartment and climbed the stairs as the fog returned. I knew I needed to lay down again and get some more sleep. It must have been around 8:00 a.m. when I passed out.

Around 4:30 p.m., I woke up again. Then, the enormity of what had happened set in as the fog finally started to lift more fully. I could see the bruises were still developing or already there; I felt the aching in my arms and legs. I still lacked a full and complete picture of what happened and never would gain a full and complete memory of those events, but I knew enough. I knew I needed to be somewhere safe and not alone, so I wandered to the safest place I could think of: my corner bar. The bartender I knew would be working that day. He and I had what can only be described as a "history." Primarily, it was a story of me trying to make him fall in love with me as much as I was undoubtedly in love with him. That effort was unsuccessful, as our "relationship" became the poster child for the word *unrequited*. Nothing had ever happened, and nothing ever would happen, but just because a passionate romance did not develop did not mean he wasn't a trusted person in my life. It was clear to me that being in that bar and drinking slowly in front of someone who knew me well was where I needed to be. It was a place where I could be around other people but also begin to process, by myself, just what the hell had happened to me the night before.

When I walked into the midnight-hued bar, only a few people were scattered about on stools and at tables. The bar had a military theme, so it resembled a scene from *M*A*S*H*: olive drab with a parachute hanging on the wall along with other samples of army decor. When the bartender caught sight of me, he stopped what he was doing, came from behind the bar and walked up to me. He put his hands on my shoulders and said, "What happened?" in the same tone a parent might when a kid comes home having gone through their worst school day ever. He knew something was terribly wrong. How he knew, I didn't really know, but I chalked it up to the fact I was a person then and today who expresses physically, mostly on my face, the best and worst of my feelings. I don't remember exactly what I said in response to his heartfelt inquiry, but the result was me sitting at the end of the bar with him rubbing my back and pouring White Russians at a healthy pace, replacing a fog I had no idea how to handle with one I was much more familiar with.

As he would leave to serve the handful of customers in the bar, a sudden clarity occurred. I was supposed to move to New York—with the person who assaulted me. I had to have three people. He was the third person. I could not do it with just two people. Here we go again. How many times can my dream be messed up in twenty-four hours? What the hell? Why was this happening to me? For just a moment, I argued with myself, likely out loud, but thankfully, there was no one else close enough to hear me.

I tried to begin an exercise in bargaining with what chunks of my memory of the last twenty-four hours remained. Maybe it was not what I thought it was. Maybe it was all a bad dream or a misunderstanding. Maybe I did something. Maybe this was all my fault. Maybe it would be okay. Maybe it was worth it to let this one bad thing go and still follow my dream. I knew others had made that sacrifice; it would be all right. Then, a different sensation came into my brain with a crescendo: bells loud enough to toll from the top of St Mary's, St Paul's, and every other sainted belfry on the planet. It was a feeling of fear—abject terror—and I realized I was shaking.

At that very moment, the door of the bar opened, and none other than my "friend," future roommate, and recently attempted rapist walked into the bar. On every single previous occasion when we had seen each other at the bar, he would immediately come up to me, say hello, and sit down. But on this one darkened June afternoon, right before he was supposed to move with me to New York, he pretended not to see me and sat down at a table less than ten feet away. It was at that moment that the whole damn truth barreled through my well-intentioned but horribly self-destructive attempts at bargaining.

I knew then. It was deliberate; he had planned it, and another suggestion from the bartender about why my memory was so foggy came back to me. According to him, I had likely been drugged at the goodbye party. Now, watching the person sitting a few feet away who likely did that and attempted to take advantage of it, rage and anger welled up inside that I had never previously felt at any point in my life. It may have been the only thing strong enough to pierce through the eerie clouds that still fogged up my conscious self.

It was all gone: not just my dream of living in New York but an innocence that had shielded me and protected me from so much of the horror and tragedy of the bigger, nastier world. My friends have always been my safety net. Working in the fire department, the devotion of the people you worked with was supposed to be infallible. I knew that even my coworkers who were not "on board" with the gay thing would never hurt me, at least not intentionally. Many of my non-fire department friends demonstrated themselves to be well-intentioned and compassionate. Yes, there had been heartbreak and anguish and my coming out journey was particularly challenging with my family, but this was different. This was as though the entire world had conspired to crush something I had been required to do by my very DNA. First, one friend backed out, and now the other had done the unthinkable.

The bartender, ever aware for professional reasons of everything going on in the bar, had noticed that individual's arrival. He had heard me say just a few minutes before what had happened. He came from behind the bar, leaned across my shoulder, and asked the question God himself would have probably asked me at that moment. I could make a case that, in that particular moment, the bartender was acting on God's behalf, summarizing God's question to Abraham: What shall you be willing to sacrifice, even in the face of an excruciating loss?

"I would rather not have my dream than have to share it with him."

That was the answer. I said it out loud. Twice. A third time. Then, I got up from the bar at the clearest moment that day had yet offered me. I walked over to where he was sitting alone at one of the high bar tables.

"I did not even see you there. How are you?" he said. I noticed he did not make eye contact.

I did not answer the question, only offered a terse instruction: "It is only because of my respect for [*the bartender*] that I am not going to make a scene, but you will walk over into the corner with me so we can have a conversation." He complied with the timidity of a scolded child. I knew then that I had been wrong before; he was fully aware of everything that had happened. Upon reaching the corner of the bar, I gave my George Patton-worthy speech in a straightforward and clear tone. In a hushed but firm voice, I expressed my anger, my frustration, and my exasperation at what he did. My concluding words were, "And if I ever see you again, I will kill you." He said nothing in response. No denial. No apology. Just left the bar. I would never see him again.

I would like to say so many years on that I did not mean it, but I think that would be a lie. I was dealing with the end of so many things at that moment. It was all broken. What was I going to do? Where was I going to go? I had no idea.

The fog came in again about that time—not the White Russian one, but the last appearance of what were likely date-rape drugs that had been put into my drinks at the bar the night before. I am pretty sure that I ate dinner somewhere, but I am not sure. I remember where I ended up that night well. It was a visit that would resuscitate my dying dream and restore the course of my life to its intersection with the City of New York, its fire department, and all those experiences would entail.

It was around 8:30 p.m. that I found myself at the door of another friend. He was a journalist. We had met on a sort of blind date where I was guilty of setting high expectations in the time before online photos were so ubiquitous. I set those high expectations by comparing myself to an actor that he loved and who, in truth, I looked nothing like at all. He would have been forgiven for casting me off because of my delusional self-image, but fortunately, that did not happen. A friendship blossomed where romance did not, and he had become a part of my circle. He even invited me to his family Christmas the year I was told it was better off not to come to my own family festivities because of, well, you know, the whole gay thing. My replacement Christmas was fine, though, and I bonded with his sister over our shared love of country music star Bryan White. I opened gifts just like I belonged, sort of like the exchange student not from another country but of another mindset. Thankfully, my family would eventually moderate their views. Still, for that first Christmas, it was probably suitable for everyone that I went a different way, and I was blessed beyond measure to have that option.

I knocked on his door, hoping he would be awake. Luckily, he was, and he opened with a "what the hell" puzzlement. I took a step into the apartment and then collapsed onto the floor. It the physical and emotional reaction to the entire event. Not just of what had happened but also of what the combination of those events meant for my future. My friend helped me to the couch, and I curled into a ball. I could not say how coherent I was, but I explained as best I could what had happened. He talked to me slowly and calmly, in reassuring tones. Most of the time, when I spoke, my eyes were closed. I was unable to process any additional input to my totally shattered self.

Finally, as the shaking abated and I started to feel a bit better, I opened my eyes and looked around the apartment. I then caught a view of the coffee table. Laying all over the top of the table were all kinds of brochures and literature about New York City. That sparked a quiet shock and then rapid-fire questions about what was happening. My friend explained that he was going to be our third person. He had decided the night before that he wanted to join us, partly to help my dream come true. I was floored. I couldn't remember if I had told him about the other guy who had potentially been the third. I know I had told him about the friend who declined at the last minute. No matter the details, it was clear at that moment that the dream was restored. The plan was revived. I started to cry. This was way too much emotion in one twenty-four-hour period. We discussed this plan a bit more, but not too much, which indicates how messed up I was.

Generally, in the face of such developments, my Virgo planning self would immediately develop and modify a three-ring binder full of tabbed pages to express the new plan of who was going to New York City and how we would make it happen.

At that moment, I realized that not more planning, but an escape or a break was needed. The day had broken me, at first in really horrible ways. In response to that horrific event, I had been comforted and supported by one friend, and another friend had single-handedly rescued my dream of moving to New York. We hatched a plan to break the cycle of the day's drama. I let my friend drive my Oldsmobile, and we went to another friend's house, where we decided to do what kids had done for years in central Ohio to escape from whatever needed escaping. We drove the entire circle of the outer belt, the fifty-four-mile loop that circles Columbus. While we drove, we sang along to the sounds of Petula Clark and managed to put some of the crazy, horrible day behind us. We sang not just "Downtown" (everyone knows that one) but the slightly more obscure but, way more New York-appropriate "Don't Sleep in the Subway" and the "Downtown" sequel, "I Know a Place."

After an hour or so of this, and thankfully, no speeding tickets or other interactions with anyone save perhaps perplexed fellow drivers, we found our way to an all-night pizza place near Ohio State's campus. An institution in the campus scene, the spot was famous for its mascot: a giant hound dog on top of a Cadillac. It was also renowned for its rather indeterminate service and that they served pizza that was more celebrated for its availability than its taste or other qualities.

Upon walking in, you could see instantly that it was a typical night. Only one stressed server, wearing the grunge college girl outfit of the times, was there. A large contingent of customers had wandered in from the now-closed bars nearby. There was a smoky glow that would seem more at home in the jazziest of basement lounges in the West Village of New York City.

After a justifiably long wait, the server approached our table and asked what we wanted in short and impatient tones. Something connected me to her. Maybe it was the day I had just been through. Perhaps it was the day she had just been through. Whatever it was, it was a spark—the kind of connection people share who have been through the same horrible event and, from that moment forward, have a bond that defies easy explanation to outsiders. Before I would answer her question about what I wanted, I made it a point to ask how she was doing. I did it directly, making eye contact. It may have been a touch creepy in any other instance. In this case, it was something a bit more. Instead of answering and with a full restaurant of customers, she just sat down, right at our booth. We all started talking. We had a two-hour conversation about life and dreams and possibilities and the shit you have to go through to get there. It was a catharsis session at a dirty booth in a late-night pizza place in the middle of everyone's worst day ever—or at least hers and mine.

Every fifteen minutes or so, I would get up and play another series of Johnny Cash selections from the jukebox. She put our pizza order in, although I am not sure anyone else in the restaurant even got a drink order filled, much less a pizza. She sat at our table, talked with us, shared our pizza, and did something I did not understand I needed. She helped bring me back into the community, continuing the work of the bartender and my friend who had announced his intention to move to New York. It was just us, the pizza, a pitcher of soda, and the slow return of feeling and awareness. It had been a tough twenty-four hours. I had been let down horribly by people who were friends. However, I had been rescued by other friends and by strangers and Johnny Cash singing from the tired speakers of a dive-bar-pizza joint anchored by a giant plastic dog. I had experienced my greatest dream dying a horrible death at the hands of a sexual predator. I came out of the other side only to be restored to my original condition at the hands of the universe or God or Petula Clark or all of it, wrapped up into the kind of crazy stew my life has always been.

I have no idea what time I made it home that night. I do not even know how I got there. It would be a few weeks before we set off for New York. There were boxes to pack, the last couple of weeks at work, and more friends to say goodbye to. I spent more time at the local bars and at my other local institution, Tommy's, a diner on West Broad Street. It is a place with the feel of something far older but was only in its sixth year when I moved. On my last lunchtime visit, as I shared with Tommy that I was leaving, he shared his terse assessment in a heavily Greek accent: "Ya not gonna like it." He said it three times—and then that was it.

A few days later, with the help of friends carrying more boxes than any studio apartment should support, we loaded the U-Haul truck and a car and were finally ready to head off. It was a journey that I probably should have made years before. It was not happening as I had initially planned. It was in the shadow of one of the most horrific experiences of my life and some of the most heartwarming intersections with friendship and love I would ever know. Whatever it was, whatever it reflected, it was happening. Our caravan departed far later than planned for the well-known combination of highways that would lead us east. We slogged through the foothills of Appalachia that make eastern Ohio a rolling green blanket, across the mud-filled Ohio River at Wheeling, West Virginia, and then into the long trek across Pennsylvania. At Carlise, we exited the Pennsylvania turnpike to Interstate 81, passing north of Harrisburg, then to I-78 into New Jersey, past the oil and chemical-filled tanks, smokestacks, and the far-off towers of Manhattan to the gateway to New York City via Staten Island: the Goethals Bridge. It took about ten hours and twenty-five and half years, but the big moment had finally arrived.

12 | GETTING SETTLED IN NYC

For my roommates and me, our mission was clear. I was moving there to take a job (eventually) with the New York City Fire Department as a fire alarm dispatcher. I took that test in April of 1999 and had scored high enough to be invited to take the job provisionally, without a permanent appointment via the civil service process. When I first received the provisional job offer in late 1999, I was not ready to take a leap of faith and move to New York without a more permanent position, so I deferred. However, by June of 2000, I was prepared to go, knowing (or at least believing) that eventually I would be offered a permanent position to join the FDNY as a fire alarm dispatcher.

Before continuing, a moment of clarification about the job title I had applied for is required. Instead of the more common "industry" terms of dispatcher or public safety communications technician, FDNY uses the term "fire alarm dispatcher" to describe the entry-level position for fire department dispatch personnel. Fire alarm dispatchers were, and remain, responsible for receiving and processing all requests for the fire department within the city of New York. Another critical difference between FDNY and most other jurisdictions in the United States is that FDNY fire dispatchers focus on fire dispatch alone. EMS and law enforcement dispatch, as well as primary call taking (answering 911 calls), are the responsibility of other New York City agencies. The "alarm" portion of the job description is simply another version of the word *incident,* because every event the Fire Department responds to is an "alarm," even if it does not come in via a fire alarm system.

Despite my excitement about being hired by FDNY, my medium- to long-term plan was to be in FDNY for a short time. It was to be a temporary stop, a placeholder, and a step in a journey to something "bigger." I wanted to work for the Fire Department long enough to get my feet wet in New York, get acclimated, settle into my new home, and then apply to graduate school. My goal was to pursue a career path in the United Nations or other global organizations as a diplomat or other international government official. My initial degree plan in college had been International Relations and Spanish. Even though I had transitioned to Urban Geography and History while at Ohio State, I had further visions of going to grad school and still following a career path much different than the fire service. I had big dreams that the FDNY was, in my mind, only a tiny part. This move to New York was the essential first step in my long-delayed effort to make those dreams come true. Simultaneously, it was a critical part of filling in the puzzle pieces about who I was and who I wanted to be.

We arrived at the end of what had been a terrible year for our landlady. Her husband had recently died, as had her son, who was the previous resident of the basement apartment. The landlady remained in the upstairs apartment as she tried to process these two devastating losses and the introduction of three guys from Ohio on the lower floors of the place where she had lived with her family. This must have been a challenging situation to work through. On paper, she was the perfect landlady for our group of three gay roommates. She had a character that defied explanation or boundaries and, in many ways, extended out into the surrounding neighborhood, where she was known as quite the character. Once, after returning from the market, we heard a loud crash upstairs. Up the open stairway, we yelled to see if she was all right. "Everything's fine," she responded, "one of the sardines not dead yet." Another evening, far into the night really, we sensed someone at the front door and found her gazing off into the distance at nothing in particular. When we asked what was going on, she replied she was just waiting for her husband to come home. We did not have the heart to remind her of the obvious. We just said something banal and wandered back into our apartment.

We almost felt guilty for being late with the rent so many times in those first few months. The temp jobs we believed we had set up fell through almost immediately. On a previous trip, we met with, and built profiles with, several temporary employment agencies in the city. Still, when we arrived and reported ready for assignments, they found it "impossible" to find work for us. As with most young people moving to the big city, none of us was quite financially stable enough to have savings to last for the months it took to manage the rent, food, and other bills necessary for every New Yorker. The stress of the move and living with two friends, when I had no relatable experience, was too much to take. In that first month, I came down with pneumonia and continued to scour want ads, trying to find a job that would pay enough to allow me to pay rent and buy food. My two roommates were more fortunate in their efforts, staying healthy and getting out to make connections and find employment relatively quickly.

The start date of the next fire alarm dispatcher class had been delayed, making my alternate job hunt more critical and necessary. This was not entirely an unexpected development but one that I had not planned for. Municipal hiring processes often work slowly and in stops and starts, impacted by budgets, civil service issues, lawsuits, and other mysterious factors. Faced with no job prospects, recovering from illness, and wondering if the FDNY would ever come through, one of those nefarious loan offer checks arrived in the mail. They are now rightfully banned because of the onerous interest rate provisions. I also had no identifiable way of paying them back, but $4,000 was $4,000, so I cashed the check as quickly as I could and prayed. It was a lifesaver and made up for the lack of income and the quickly dwindling savings I had set aside before the move.

Shortly after I took the loan, the Fire Department announced they were again delaying my new hire class's start date from September to December. Panic quickly escalated to desperation, and in an event much like the finding of my apartment in Columbus, a tiny newspaper ad for a temp agency led me to a phone call and a new employment possibility. In the meantime, my original temp firm finally came up with an assignment, working as an administrative assistant in various offices of Chase Bank in Manhattan. Over the next month or two, I worked at various locations in Lower Manhattan and at 270 Park Avenue, the Chase World Headquarters. I was trying to slowly build a path out of the financial chasm that moving to New York had led me into. The wages were terrible, but at least they were wages, and I had enough money to eat and barely pay the rent for our palatial home in Brooklyn. Along the way, cheap slices of pizza and street vendor hot dogs became a way of life, enhanced by occasional jaunts to White Castle. It was all about living cheaply, but certainly not elegantly.

My turning point toward salvation would appear in the form of the new temporary employment service I applied to. When I interviewed, the assignment coordinator took a liking to me and offered me a work assignment for the princely sum of $17 per hour. It was substantially more than I had been making, so I enthusiastically made my way to my assignment with an engineering firm located near Penn Station. My job, as near as I could tell, was to be an executive assistant to the manager of their travel department. She was a larger-than-life human being with enough personality to fill the entirety of the fifty-story building where I now worked. She had a massive ring on her finger that I asked her about one day. Her response said it all: "The only thing my husband ever got me worth anything was this ring. I don't know where he is today, but I know where the ring is."

The assignment was perfect for me as the most crucial part of my day was keeping her company, often while she called partners or vendors and yelled at them in a classic part-Southern, part-Creole with a side of honey-soaked tirade. I loved every minute of that assignment, so much so that when I completed the fire department training schedule, I returned to the role as a side job. Doing those two jobs together was the chance to get my head above water financially, which turned the tide. Given my less-than-stellar scores on technical skills assessments around Word, Excel, and other office software tools, and my inability to do most other typical administrative tasks, it was a shock that I had been hired for a temp office admin job in the first place, much less invited back. Along the way, I learned the valuable truth about qualifications. Sometimes, they are overrated. If you engage with people, make them feel special, show the right attitude, and do the best at whatever you can do, sometimes opportunities present themselves that are perhaps not in your area, but are enough to keep the lights on until something else comes along. The real chance would finally present itself on December 4, 2000, the day I started my FDNY fire alarm dispatcher career.

During the fall of 2000, while I worked at the temp job and things became more comfortable financially and spiritually, I started genuinely getting to know my new home. I was finding places I would integrate into my rituals. An Italian restaurant in the East Village, various bars, coffee shops, and bookstores became my regular haunts. One of my favorite bookstores in the city was a branch of the now long-defunct Borders bookstore chain, located at Five World Trade Center in Lower Manhattan on the eastern edge of the World Trade Center Complex. I also started hanging out at the Cubbyhole regularly, making friends with the other regulars, but never again running into the fairy godmother who had treated me to the tour of the city the year before. While exploring, I made it a point to learn the city geography in advance of my new job. I knew from my previous experience that being an effective dispatcher demands you expertly know the area you are responsible for as well as the locations of the fire stations and apparatus that are, in effect, the tools in your toolbox.

In addition to working my day job and exploring the city along with my roommates, we set about building a network of friends and trying our hand at dating. The experience of dating in a new city, especially one as massive, complex, and simultaneously intricate as New York, was challenging at best and terrifying at worst. However, we made our way through and even found some steady relationships to help keep us company.

My focus, however, was more on getting comfortable in my life in the city than in a serious romantic entanglement, even though I wouldn't consciously understand that until years later. As a result, I dated some really decent people who might have made good long-term partners, but my head and heart, especially in those early days of living in the big city, were not in the space of building something extremely serious. Owing to the extreme social nature of one of my roommates, before long we had enough friends to host a spectacular party in our apartment with somewhere north of fifty guests, including musical entertainment from a relatively well-known New York City drag queen. We called the party the "Queens of Kings County," and it remains one of the best social experiences of my life and certainly one of the best of my time in New York. When a rendition of Liza Minnelli's "Ring Them Bells" brought down the house, it felt like we were home—truly home—and only five short months after we had arrived.

Everything felt in front of us then, as though the move to the city was not just the best decision ever but a decision that was going to be smooth and easy from that point. To any knowledgeable outsider, that view would have been considered a fallacy. By the end of our first year in New York, about six months from the night of the epic party, we would all be splitting up as roommates. One, the person who saved my dream by surprising me the night of the assault with the news he would join us, would move to the opposite end of the city. Our friendship faded into the mist of space and time and the side effects of much different ways of living. Sometimes people just grow apart, but it was sad to feel that friendship float away. My other roommate, the person who was the life of the party, would also find his way out of our shared life. He had a romantic partner from the other side of the country who he moved to be with and then shortly after abandoned, moving back to Columbus just before September 11, 2001. The following years would be tough on him as he fell entirely into the demons that tortured him just below and above the surface of his charming personality. I had seen those demons but always held out hope that they would prove manageable. They did not. We, too, fell out of touch, only for me to run into him several years later when I was back in Columbus for my mother's funeral.

Some friends and I stopped by that same neighborhood bar that had been my refuge years before and ran into him there. As he spoke in a manic stream of pleasantries, he was shaking uncontrollably. His eyes were sunken and marked the type of vacant and distant presence of someone consumed by drugs. That evening was the last time I saw him alive. Years later, prompted by someone asking me what had happened to him, I searched for his name online. It's an indictment of sorts that sometimes we find out what happens to people who were once so important in our lives by searching the Internet. On the night we searched, I quickly received an answer. He had died, alone, of an overdose just a few weeks after I had seen him. I had been too consumed in the loss of my mother when I had seen him to offer much more than a "hey, reach out to me please," which was like throwing a drink umbrella to someone in need of a parachute. I feel guilty to this day. Maybe there was something more I could have done. Perhaps I could have fought harder for him to stay in New York or not invited him to go in the first place. Those questions can haunt you after the loss of a friend, especially someone who was such an essential part of your own personal story. The wiser voice in me knows that nothing could be done. However, wiser voices are not the only ones that echo in your mind on the quiet nights when you recall everything and everyone who contributed to your journey and your present life.

By the time the summer of 2001 rolled around, everything had changed from the months before. I had found a new apartment, settled into my new role with the FDNY, and figured out how, at least a little, to make New York City my home. That process, as with so much else about that time, would be completely upended by the events of September, a time when I was simply looking forward to my birthday.

13 | FOUNDATIONS AND BEGINNINGS

The New York City Fire Department is more than just an organization, or even a fire department. It occupies a storied position in the fire service and the general population as the prime firefighting department by which all others are measured. As with all things, the truth is probably somewhat different, but even its name symbolizes just how unique it is in the pantheon of public safety agencies. It is the only fire department in the United States known by a reversed acronym: FDNY. It was always said that the FD came first because the Fire Department existed long before the city it now serves.

The FDNY, as it exists today, can be traced back to 1865. The city of New York, as we know it today, can be traced to an election in 1897, when a number of voters in areas today known as the Bronx, Brooklyn, Staten Island, and Queens voted to become part of the city of New York. Residents of even more distant areas upstate and on Long Island rejected the chance to become part of New York City. As a result, the boundaries of New York today were primarily set on January 1, 1898, when the results of that election were enacted. The echoes and shadows of those merged communities are still visible today. A few of the FDNY firehouses in service still say BFD above their doors, where the B stands for the Brooklyn Fire Department. A few others were built for volunteers years before career firefighters would occupy those buildings. A surprising number of the firehouses still protecting New Yorkers were built for horse-drawn fire apparatus. (The stalls and haylofts were long ago converted to uses more befitting motorized fire protection.)

However, it is not enough just to have a fire department. Unless the fire happens to be next door to the station, some system of reporting fires had to be developed. That system in New York and many other American cities was the fire pull box, connected to a central monitoring office and the fire stations by telegraph. This system pre-dated the arrival of the telephone by a couple of decades, coming online in New York City in 1855. Initially, the system was not overly complex. Pulled boxes, located at about every other city intersection, would cause an alarm ring in firehouses. The firefighters would respond, investigate, put out the fire, and then return to their firehouse.

As the size of the city increased, the number of boxes and firehouses did as well. It became necessary to manage all these resources. It could not be done from the field, as there was no way for units to communicate with each other once they were out of a firehouse. Not until they arrived on the scene could they exchange commands and information verbally or back to the dispatchers in the central office using a telegraph key inside the boxes. Even though they were in their firehouse, the units in the field only had a limited view of the bigger picture. As a result of this need for overall command and control, a new position was created that would evolve into today's FDNY fire alarm dispatcher.

As their most important task, the initial fire alarm dispatchers monitored the circuits, bells, and boxes that comprised the city's fire reporting system. This system was the city's emergency reporting circulatory system. Defects in the system needed to be quickly identified and fixed to ensure the public could access fire department assistance when required. One indication of the role of fire alarm dispatchers was their identification as electrical workers for union purposes until the establishment of their own union as the Uniformed Fire Alarm Dispatchers Benevolent Association. Today, their affiliation with the International Association of Firefighters indicates their outsized importance to fire operations more than traditional 911 personnel.

Equally important to the system's more public-facing capabilities were the department's internal communications, incident, and unit management processes. A complicated language of codes and signals was developed, permitting the department to operate effectively without voice communication. Numbers and pauses, organized in predetermined sequences and transmitted either by dispatchers or units in the field or in quarters over the telegraph system, served as the department's high-speed coordination and communication system. These appear today in the shorthand codes the fire department uses to describe its responses and operations.

For example, today's listeners to FDNY radio dispatchers will hear the term "five-seven-signal" which traces its origins back to the telegraph days when "five" was the code for an engine company and "seven" the code for a "ladder" company. Putting them together without a pause, as in "57," followed by a pause and then a three- or four-digit number indicated that the first due engine company and first due ladder company were to respond to the indicated box number's location. Today, that same phrasing is used to describe an incident that requires the response of one engine and ladder company, even though the dispatch occurs over computer wires—not the sounding of bells. Additional combinations of numbers were used for response instructions, identification of units, and even the act of boroughs borrowing fire resources from each other in response to a major incident or to move into empty firehouses. One more duty of this code system was to share departmental announcements. Once the department deployed radio and intercom systems, these announcements would be preceded by the signal "65-2," indicating an impending departmental message.

However intricate and cumbersome these signals appear today, they were essential tools of communication in a world that existed before phones and long before radio. They were also helpful, efficient and ensured that dispatchers, firefighters, and officers were all on the same page. Companies would hear the tapping out of box numbers pulled by citizens and know immediately they were due to respond on that box. They also knew that for other boxes in other parts of the city, they may be expected to respond on the second alarm or to move up to another firehouse to provide coverage for additional incidents in the same area. The entire system demanded serious attention to detail, knowledge of geography, and proficiency in the language and code of the fire department. At the center of it all were the dispatchers.

By having everyone on the same system and aware of the ongoing fire department operations in their boroughs, the department was able to create and maintain a culture of ownership and understanding. Fire alarm dispatchers played the role of circus ringmasters or orchestra conductors. Ultimately, the fire alarm dispatchers were responsible for always ensuring that everything functioned correctly. This significant amount of responsibility necessitated an equally significant amount of authority. Still, this system of operation would prove highly effective at managing the increasingly significant amounts of activity experienced by the FDNY starting in the 1960s and continuing to the present day.

The first FDNY engine company to ever break one thousand runs (or responses) in a single year was Engine-231 in Brownsville, Brooklyn, in the early 1960s. But a mere decade later, as described vividly by the late retired FDNY firefighter Dennis Smith in his seminal book *Report from Engine Company 82*, during the 1970s multiple companies in the same firehouse in numerous neighborhoods across the city responded to five thousand runs a year or more. Those years were marked by social and political challenges, as well as incredible amounts of arson committed by frustrated residents, horrific landlords, and exacerbated by a reduction in fire department resources. Managing it all were the FDNY Fire Alarm Dispatchers. They became proud and proficient in their skill, knowledge, and abilities. They were also passionate about creating an organizational culture that continued their success.

At that time, FDNY Dispatchers worked in one of the five central offices. These buildings, one per borough, were constructed in parks to mitigate threats from conflagration or other large-scale disasters. They were designed to be self-sufficient and served as the hub of the firebox and telegraph system for each borough and the coordination point for the fire department's activities. Their decentralized nature meant that each developed a character and personality that continues to the present-day FDNY even though the former dedicated FDNY dispatch facilities have been replaced by col-located Public Safety Answering Centers shared with NYPD, FDNY EMS, and 9-1-1.

Despite the variations and nuances that can develop in such an operation, one function united the entire department—dispatcher and firefighter alike. The announcement of the *"four fives."* This telegraph signal instructed firehouses across the city to lower their flags to half-staff due to the line-of-duty death of a member. It could be used for the military death of a department member as well, but most often, its transmission was related to the loss of a member or members from a fire or other incident. In time, when voice communication became possible over the firehouse intercom system and the department radio, a verbal announcement would include the particulars of who had been lost and the basic details of the incident. This reading of the *"four fives"* would be performed by a fire alarm dispatcher and serve as a formal announcement for informational purposes. It also started a period of mourning and remembrance that would culminate with the solemnity of an official fire department line-of-duty funeral.

The Fire Department of New York and its dispatchers had primarily operated in much the same way for decades as my time with them approached. The fact that the policies and procedures, behaviors, patterns, and habits could trace their purpose back so many years gave the agency a foundation that is rare among organizations. It's often joked that departments with such a history can be slow to change or even resistant to progress. Despite those jokes, there is something good about stability and permanence, especially in an organization with such a mission-critical role. The fact that the department did not change easily also meant it did not change lightly. There were indeed discussions about the human elements and consequences of those traditions, especially as we gained awareness and understanding of the power of diversity, equity, inclusion, and belonging in organizations. However, there is also power in being on a team that knew what it stood for, what its role was, and its responsibility to manage the response to fires and emergencies in the city of New York.

When I walked through the door as a new member of that organization in the year 2000, it was comforting to know that I was part of something with such a long tradition. As one of my former coworkers used to say, working at the FDNY was like playing for the Yankees. I always thought that was a bit of a stretch, but over time, I would see firsthand what it meant to play for one of the greatest teams on one of the most historic days and one of the most inspiring and visible stages. I would come to know firsthand the power of a team when it knows who it is and what it is doing. I would come to see the importance of tradition in helping not just a fire department but an entire community, and even the world as a whole. That tradition would help us overcome not just September 11, 2001, but a variety of other days that would challenge the department, the city, and many more people in so many more places. I would come to appreciate what it means to live into a past that was imperfect with a team of crazy people who were like characters from some forgotten late-night cable show. I would become a fierce defender of all that being a part of the FDNY meant. First, I would have to learn how to make coffee.

14 | TRAINING AND ONBOARDING

In the year 2000, the FDNY commemorated the 135th year of its existence and, in many ways, was operating much the way it had since the beginning. The primary organization was the over 350 firefighting units that protected the over eight million residents of the city of New York. Those residents lived in over three hundred square miles of land divided into five boroughs. What most people know as New York City is actually one of those boroughs: Manhattan. Manhattan is where many of the most famous parts of New York City are found, where most of the visitors focus their time, and where the attention of the world's media can be captured in a moment, should that be the intentions of a terrorist attacker.

At the time, the largest borough in population was Brooklyn, located on the very western end of Long Island. The largest borough by area was and remains Queens. It is home to both of New York City's major airports and one of the largest Chinese communities in America, much larger than the more famous and more popular Chinatown in Manhattan. The Chinatown of Flushing, Queens is only one element of America's most diverse county in America's most dynamic city. Physically above Queens and Manhattan is the Bronx, where the Yankees play baseball and the extremes of New York City life exist just a few miles away from each other. The multi-million-dollar, almost idyllic suburban homes of Riverdale, the New England-style fishing community of City Island, and some of the city's poorest sections are all within a few miles as the crows, or pigeons, fly. The final borough of New York City is Staten Island. In many ways, it is the most unique compared to the other boroughs. Home to far more suburban-style landscape and construction than any of the other boroughs, it feels out of place as part of New York, which its more rightward leaning voting records and the giant shopping mall lifted straight out of the Midwest at its center seem to indicate.

Protecting this conglomeration of population and structures, residents, and visitors required the FDNY to ensure effective response times to reported fires. That required heavy staffing of its fire companies, and very well-trained dispatchers to manage it all. Over two hundred engine companies, one hundred forty ladder companies, and forty-nine battalion chiefs were the primary response units in 2000. Many other units, including rescue and squad companies that performed the most daring rescues at fires and other emergencies, as well as more typical firefighting duties, supplemented these companies. These companies were the elite of the fire department. September 11 would be a disaster for every department member, but even deadlier for those who worked in these special units.

To help ensure an appropriate and adequate response to incidents along with the management of fire department resources, FDNY still maintained five borough-based central offices in 2000. These facilities had been updated at various points in their lifespans, with some newer technologies introduced that improved the effectiveness of the operation.

No technology had a more critical impact on the operations of FDNY and its dispatchers than the computer-assisted dispatch system (CAD) known as Starfire. It is a homegrown system dedicated to FDNY needs. Introduced in the late 1970s after years of research, study, and development, this system allowed dispatchers to reduce the use of, and eventually eliminate the telegraph system and silence the bells that had sounded for over one hundred years. Dispatching units could be accomplished literally with the push of a button. Advanced for its time, the Starfire system was based mainly on the historic operational patterns of the department but with a modern touch. Companies would no longer be alerted by bells or a voice over an intercom, but rather by a computer that initiated two-tone alerts followed by an automated voice announcing which apparatus in the station should respond. The firefighter on house watch would review the accompanying computer printout, announce who was going and where, and the unit would respond. The system worked well and was extremely fast. It had been designed based on the experiences of FDNY during the "war years," the period of extreme fire activity that began in the late 1960s and continued into the 1970s. During those years, the department responded to thousands of fires each year, and the CAD system was designed to support that level of activity.

This computer system and its dispatch processes were ingrained in the culture of the FDNY and, by the year 2000, were firmly cemented as essential tools of the fire department. That legacy CAD system was only replaced in the last few years, by another custom-built CAD system called FireCAD, which builds on the legacy of that original system. Although they were important and the tools and technology remain critical to the department's mission, those tools were never as crucial as the people who operated those pieces of equipment. The training, skills, and knowledge of the professionals on both sides of the radio, in the dispatch office, and on the companies that would respond to scenes, were the primary tools of the fire department, as they are in any effective organization.

That was why the department effectively mitigated the blackout of 2003 and so many other events that would have exceeded the management capability of many other organizations. No matter what an agency's plans for large-scale disasters are or their assumptions of what should happen when facing a crisis, it comes down to the capability of the people tasked with implementing the plan and getting results. Even given the best tools, unsatisfactory leaders or team members will not find success any more than a novice piano player can wow an audience with a Steinway grand piano. However, the reverse will not necessarily bring failure. That same piano may be out of tune or even missing a key or two, but the best performers can still use it to make spectacular music.

Such is the way with organizations; it starts and ends with people. When those people are empowered and trained, know what role they have to play, and are held to a standard everyone understands equally, they can play the most beautiful music imaginable. They can dispatch, respond to, and mitigate emergencies and fires well beyond the ordinary course of business or even the most demanding "once-in-a-lifetime" events. To be clear, almost all dispatch organizations will find a way through the hardest of days eventually. Quite a few agencies are capable of handling extreme events, especially those that experience hurricanes and tornadoes with tragic frequency. However, the level of consistent performance that must be demonstrated by FDNY fire alarm dispatchers, and the degree to which those personnel are responsible for effective department operations in all conditions, is largely unique in the profession and in its impact on all sorts of crazy and normal days.

Training for newly hired dispatchers includes a first day of orientation at Fire Department headquarters in downtown Brooklyn. That is the day to fill out the paperwork, get ID cards, and handle all the administrative tasks associated with a new city job. It was also an opportunity for FDNY leadership to share their insight about the job and what was expected regarding performance as a new dispatcher. I was hired into a class of nine other dispatchers. Several moved over from the New York City Police Department, where they had served as 911 call takers and police radio dispatchers. A couple of other classmates were volunteer firefighters, and one came from a health system dispatch office.

Each person in the class brought unique gifts and experiences to his or her new role in the fire department. The dispatchers from the police department were comfortable being very busy. The radio dispatchers for NYPD are some of the busiest in the world. They manage massive amounts of activity with a terse proficiency that matches the exact needs of a busy public safety organization, whether a police department or a fire department. The volunteer firefighters in the class were able to bring their experience of responding to fires and emergencies in their communities and help expand the overall understanding of the group, even though they had essentially never been in the dispatch center. It was a wonderful blend of previous skills and awareness and a valuable opportunity for each class member to share his or her unique talents for the greater good. In this environment where everyone wants to succeed, the essential factors for completion are attitude and effort. It is up to each individual to decide if he or she wants to rise to the standard of training and performance required to continue into the subsequent phases of dispatcher training, or if he or she is just not the right fit for the department.

In the face of the standards, traditions, and expectations, I was the only person from outside New York in the class, which immediately made me feel like an outsider. I also assumed I was the only gay person in the class. Being the double outsider was a bit more complicated than I expected. So I decided to focus first on the job and then figure out how, or if, to come out. I had used that same approach before, although not with quite as much intention. It had worked out well, so I figured I should apply the same plan.

The decision to take that approach took work, however. There had been significant internal debate about how much of my identity to offer to my classmates. Although New York was a progressive place, its fire department, like any other big city public safety organization, was not, in my assumption, as open and affirming as its population. As an outsider, both in terms of geography and sexual orientation and seriously wanting to prove myself as a dispatcher before identifying myself as a particular class, I held back revealing too much about who I was. I decided to save those conversations for later, once I made my way through training and could figure out who I could talk to about it. I would not wait long, but I wanted to be strategic about it.

I threw myself into the class work and into making sure that I was the most knowledgeable person I could be. I tried too hard, pressured myself too much, and thought I would earn respect by being perfect. Nothing like setting yourself up to fail from minute one. It was not until I backed off a little and started to feel the hints of that earlier burnout from Ohio State returning that I started to really enjoy what I was doing and started bonding with my classmates. Owing to the nature of the job, training was difficult and not everyone made it to the end of module one. By the time this first phase of training ended, which focused on call taking and notifications, only six of the ten members of the initial class remained.

The coursework had been intense, with daily quizzes on department operations. We took weekly field trips to the dispatch offices, where we practiced our developing skills on live callers while being observed by members of the training unit. This is where the native New Yorkers had an advantage over me. The special language of New Yorkers is even more unique when they are screaming on a phone reporting an emergency or fire. Translating what they said required not just excellent hearing but also a forceful and direct approach to asking the caller the right questions to get that information. We handled every single call the same way, asking the same six questions followed by a standard ending statement. This script was designed to ensure we were able to meet our primary objective: getting the call answered and processed with the right information in the least amount of time. Time was of the essence, owing to the tendency of fires to grow significantly the longer they burn. Fire in New York City was dangerous not just to property but to the lives of citizens, visitors, and firefighters. There was no time to delay or fool around. Further, the technology of the time was not advanced enough to support getting the information that a caller could not or would not provide. Before the advent of cellphones, if the caller was calling from a landline phone this process was easier. Landline calls to 9-1-1 generally included the address of where the phone was registered and the assigned telephone number. Cellphone calls did not provide much beyond the call-back number and a very generalized location which could be off by a degree of miles from where the caller was actually physically located. Even landlines were limited in their location support, especially when language barriers existed between the dispatcher and the caller, when the caller is reporting someone else's emergency or they did not remain on the phone to talk to us when transferred by the police department 9-1-1 call-taker. In total, the process of ascertaining just where a fire or emergency was occurring was surprisingly difficult and, in many ways, the most challenging part of the job.

The second most challenging part was consistently learning the nuances and unwritten rules that governed your daily activities on the floor. Some of the senior dispatchers were engaging and more than willing to help out the newer dispatchers. Others preferred you not even talk to them for at least a few years—at least until you had proven yourself. Coffee fell into that area of nuance. It was not a written rule but expectation that keeping coffee pots filled, going out to pick up food orders, and helping keep up the CO's appearance was part of your job. Yes, there were cleaners who did the big stuff, but keeping the Central Office as neat as it could be was the purview of the junior dispatchers on shift, second only in importance to learning how to do the job—well.

Despite the inherent challenges, new FDNY dispatchers quickly become adept at getting essential information and picking up clues indicating the crucial details of an incident. Sounds of breaking glass and screaming bystanders almost always indicate a particularly serious fire. A child laughing into the phone or street corner ERS (Emergency Reporting System) box and reporting a fire at 3:00 p.m. (as school let out) is almost always a false alarm. Specific neighborhoods or particular addresses are famous for food-on-the-stove fires and stuck elevators. In contrast, phone calls for fires after midnight always necessitate special attention, especially if they come from areas that do not often experience fires. This is the type of insight FDNY dispatchers quickly developed in their time on the job.

We were busy, and every fire provided lessons to be integrated into our experience. That part of the job is even more critical because of the position of the dispatcher in the FDNY hierarchy.

In many other cities, responding chiefs make almost all the decisions about responses, additional units, and moving units to higher priority incidents. In New York, those responsibilities fall upon the fire dispatchers. That reflects the lessons learned during periods of heightened activity. It is impossible for a chief in the field to make the best possible decisions about resource management and utilization without having a view of all the incidents that are in progress, information about unit availability and all the other factors that impact just what units go where and when. Further, having the dispatchers responsible for these tasks frees up the Chief Officers to manage their incidents and fires and focus on the tasks that only they are positioned to do well. FDNY fire dispatchers have significant leverage to redeploy resources, modify responses, and in essence serve as the incident commander of events until the on-scene arrival of an actual fire officer. However, the other side of that much authority was the amount of training, education, knowledge, and experience needed for someone to be good at the job. Therefore, approximately 50 percent of new hires washed out in their first portions of training. Another percentage washed out in the second and third training modules that focused on radio operations, firehouse communications, and overall dispatching and resource management. It was not an easy process to learn all that information. However, I can confess that its intricacy was something I found seriously fascinating. It suited me very well then and I still recall, years later, a sizable chunk of my dispatcher training.

Another reason this system worked was that each of the five FDNY communications offices functioned as a team. Although there were five different "roles" filled by personnel on a shift, everyone always needed to be aware of what was happening operationally. The floorplan of the positions, the single radio frequency for the units to communicate with the dispatcher that was broadcast aloud for everyone in the building to hear, and the dispatcher "voices" of call-takers answering alarms meant that you could, with time, develop the ability to follow along with everything going on in the dispatch office and in the field. Being on the same page also helped ensure everyone looked out for one another. If someone heard a mistake or a question, he or she would not hesitate to say something. If a dispatcher on the radio heard a call taker talking with a caller about people trapped in a second-floor bedroom, the dispatcher would relay that information to the units responding verbally. This ensured that the information pathway was streamlined and that the occupants had the best chance of being rescued. There were even almost daily instances where the quality of information provided by a caller was so descriptive, it motivated the dispatchers to redirect units from other incidents to these higher priority events. This resulted in response times of seconds instead of minutes, thereby saving lives. These were not rare occurrences; they were expected parts of job performance of every fire alarm dispatcher.

Critically, these elevated decisions and adjustments were not on the orders of the dispatch supervisor. The dispatch supervisor was there primarily to supervise, not do the everyday work of the dispatchers. She or he was responsible for catching issues with responses and staffing, maintaining a journal of activities, and a variety of other tasks focused on the status of the building, the fire alarm box system, and interactions with management.

The group of dispatchers working the shift "ran the borough," with the fire alarm dispatcher assigned to the decision dispatcher role serving as coordinator of all dispatch operations. That person could have as little as six or seven months on the job. As terrifying as that may sound to some, it worked, and it worked well because of the system of operational awareness and the amount of knowledge and skill that every member of the team would possess. Other dispatchers would be assigned to the Radio-In and Radio-Out positions, the Voice Alarm/ Notification position, and as Alarm Receipt Dispatchers (Call-takers).

Once released from training, I was assigned to the Brooklyn Central Office on Empire Boulevard and Washington Avenue. Just across the street were the Ebbets Field Houses, a housing project on the previous site of the stadium where the Brooklyn Dodgers had played baseball until their move to Los Angeles in 1958. History was never far from any place in the FDNY, and that was reflected in our own building. Between its completion and opening as the Fire Department Dispatch Center for Brooklyn, the worst subway disaster in the city's history occurred just behind that building.

In 1918, a subway train operated by a replacement motorman during a subway worker's strike crashed into a newly constructed bridge while traveling at excessive speed through a curve. Nearly one hundred passengers were killed. The elegant, newly completed but not yet equipped and occupied city-owned building next to the site served as a temporary morgue. Stories of the ghosts who still haunt the building greeted me on my arrival. Even though I never saw an actual ghost, I did have more than a few strange sensations and visions late at night in the building, as did almost everyone who worked there. One notable vision was of a lady in period clothing walking silently in the basement hall, but it was late, and I was tired, so I assumed it was just a waking dream.

The transition to the platform was made easier by my supervisor and a passionate group of fellow younger dispatchers, most of whom would later leave dispatch to become FDNY firefighters. During my time at FDNY, that became a persistent career path for others. Becoming a firefighter was lengthy and highly competitive, and the timeline was slightly more accessible for those who had started as dispatchers. Although it was an excellent opportunity for those who wanted to become firefighters, it did have the unfortunate side effect of creating a revolving door situation. Dispatchers who had become good at the job left to go to the "other side" and were replaced by new groups of potential firefighters following the same path.

Over the following months, I would practice my call-taking skills and be introduced to the other working positions in the office, getting the chance to sit and practice them even before I had been sent for formal training. I also discovered the flaw in my plan of managing my coming out when my co-workers uncovered my AOL chat profile and some of the details contained within. I don't know why it never occurred to me that they would find it. AOL chat was a big thing back then, so it should not have been surprising. Maybe it was a subconscious way to come out without any drama of a big announcement. What was surprising to me was how that revelation was handled. As I was told by another new dispatcher, on a night that I was off, how to handle it became the topic of conversation for the entire shift. The entire tour (seven dispatchers) debated back and forth the proper course of action for the now double outsider in their midst. The supervisor, a long-time member of the department and well-respected senior statesman, made it perfectly clear to everyone that it would not be an issue and that what I did as a dispatcher was what would matter. That ended the discussion. No one would ever say a single cross thing directly to me about the issue as long as I was in the department.

That did not mean, of course, that things were not said behind my back or that I was not given grief about certain things, especially about being from Ohio. Still, it was never in a way different than how everyone else grief about things. I was never made to feel like an "other" because of who I was. That was an indescribable gift for an out-of-town outsider, who also felt like a gay outsider, in a fire department regarded as the most traditional in the United States, if not the world.

It is a badge of honor to admit that I would later run into issues, not because of my orientation, but because of my resistance to that tradition and my desire to do things in new and different ways. This created discomfort for some of the old guard. However, in all of those experiences, some of which would be positive, some of which would be negative, I never felt targeted or singled out for my sexual orientation.

A further indication of my ability to succeed in the department was my career path, which led me to be promoted through the rank structure. I ultimately became Director of FDNY Fire Dispatch Operations in 2014. In each of the roles I served, I was fortunate to have wonderful groups of people working alongside me, who helped make the challenges of the various jobs more manageable than they might have been. Leading an organization of two hundred people, or even supervising a few members of that organization, is not an easy job, even if it is made easier by the professionalism of your colleagues. While serving in those roles, whether as supervisor, training coordinator, chief dispatcher, deputy director, or director, I was able to learn the most important lessons of my professional career. Every lesson and every insight were based on real-world incidents and real-life administrative challenges in a mission-critical organization of talented and skilled human beings living and working in America's greatest city. It was an environment perfect for learning and growing, for getting some things right and many more wrong.

15 | SUMMER OF 2001

By the time September of 2001 rolled around, I was well into my first year as a fire alarm dispatcher and more fully adjusting to the pace and life of being in New York City. The regular working schedule was unique and permitted a great deal of off time for adventures in the city. While "on the chart," dispatchers and supervisors worked two twelve-hour day shifts followed by twenty-four hours off and then two twelve-hour night shifts, followed by either four or five days off. I had completed two thirds of my formal training. I was certified to take phone calls and make notifications to outside entities, do call-backs for more information about incidents, and also work the radio-in, radio-out, and voice-alarm positions. These three positions were the "voice" of the fire department.

Once fully trained, dispatchers rotated among each of the five working positions in the central office. The other two were the alarm receipt dispatcher (ARD, or call-taker) and the decision dispatcher. The alarm receipt position was the first that new dispatchers were trained to operate. At most times, each of the five boroughs would have between two or three ARDs on duty. These personnel would answer the inbound phone calls for fire department assistance and help out with other tasks around the office as needed. The last position, decision dispatcher, served as a floor manager. This person reviewed each of the incidents entered by ARDs or arriving from direct computer links, verified the proper response was recommended by the Computer Assisted Dispatch (CAD) system, and then "released" alarms to the units assigned to respond. At that point, the voice alarm dispatcher would have to notify the designated firehouses if, for some reason, their in-house printers and/or speakers were not operational. Once the units acknowledged their dispatch, the radio-out dispatcher announced the run, and the response process began. If you are listening to FDNY radio today, multi-company incidents are announced about seventy-five seconds after all units have acknowledged their runs. Single company runs are generally not announced on the radio unless a unit fails to respond to their mobile data computer (MDC) indicating they have a response. This is one of the ways FDNY was well ahead of its time. They pioneered a concept called "voiceless" dispatch many years before the term became popular.

Beyond the direct communications systems, we also had various other devices and systems that beeped, chimed, and whirred. There was a dot-matrix printer that spat out a report every five minutes. This was a snapshot of the status of any active unit in the borough. This would be used to document where units were in the case our main computer suffered a hiccup. In addition, a similar printer sat near the radio and provided a paper copy of the incidents as they were transmitted, again in case there was a system failure, and the radio dispatchers needed an immediate paper copy of an incident.

From your first day "on the floor," you were expected to become a master of your borough's geography, the operational policies and procedures of the department, and to learn about fireground operations. You needed to have reasonable expectations of what was occurring across your borough no matter how busy it became. Those who responded to the scene aided in this responsibility. The policy and procedure around information shared by the first unit arriving, as well as the information shared in regular updates from the incident commander at serious incidents, were essential elements of managing not just that particular event, but they also helped the dispatcher understand the likely resource impacts to his or her borough and potentially, the entire city.

All these details, information, and reports as well as the need to integrate that mountain of information into your actions as a dispatcher made it extremely challenging. In some ways, it was even more difficult the longer you were on the job and began to more fully appreciate everything going on around you. That was why the training process was broken down into bite-sized chunks. Throwing new personnel into the pool's deep end from their first day on the job would likely have been far too overwhelming.

Despite the module approach and the help of classmates and co-workers, by summer, only five of the ten folks I had come on the job with remained. The five of us became part of a two-hundred-person organization. Of these, about thirty dispatchers would be working across the city at any one time, spread across the five borough offices. In each of the five offices, a supervising dispatcher was in charge. Together, this team was responsible for fire responses in their borough and coordinating with other borough offices as circumstances required. We would also coordinate and communicate with FDNY's emergency medical services dispatchers as needed. A separate team of professionals handled EMS dispatch. They were part of the fire department but had their own facilities, policies, and procedures. Their workforce was made up of line EMTs and paramedics who were assigned to that role instead of, or in addition to, working in the field. Their facility at the time was located in downtown Brooklyn, not far from Fire Department headquarters and the foot of the Brooklyn Bridge. Although both groups were part of the FDNY at a high level, they would not become physically co-located until about a decade after 9/11.

The third element of the public safety dispatching system was that of the NYPD. This very busy operation, staffed with hundreds of NYPD civilian employees, was housed in a communications center in downtown Brooklyn, near the one maintained by EMS. They were (and remain) the primary answering point for 911 calls in the city of New York and the radio dispatchers for NYPD. They answered 911 calls first and processed law enforcement emergencies. Medical emergencies were conferenced (or transferred) to EMD (for medical emergencies) and fire emergencies to the FDNY Central Office of the respective borough. For events requiring multiple agencies, a computer link existed to share information. However, despite this link, the primary goal was always to get a call-taker from FDNY Fire Dispatch or Emergency Medical Dispatch on the line for fire or medical related emergencies when a caller was available.

Although my formal responsibility at work was for the borough of Brooklyn, all five communications offices, by way of their radio and CAD systems (Starfire), operated as part of one system. One borough could enter runs for other boroughs, a frequent occurrence when another borough became overloaded with calls. FDNY field units could switch radio frequencies to communicate with other dispatchers should they respond to events outside their normal area. This happened frequently in border areas, such as Greenpoint in Brooklyn or Lower Manhattan, and it involved the bridges and tunnels connecting the boroughs. Additionally, FDNY COs often borrowed units from each other for coverage needs, especially in the case of large fires or incidents that stripped entire sections of the primary borough of available units.

Over my first months on the job, and especially in the face of how he had shut down any controversy over my "coming out" on the job, my supervising dispatcher took on a God-like quality to me. Operationally, I found every one of the supervisors I encountered on the job to be intimidating but also inspirational. They each conveyed a level of skill and knowledge that set a high bar for me to meet. Indeed, there were variations, but FDNY supervising dispatchers operated with a calm, cool, and assured presence that was clearly a side effect of their experience and knowledge. Seeing these supervisors operate, especially in the face of days that exceeded the normal, was like watching jazz masters perform.

My first supervisor was one of the best bosses I would ever have in any job. He expressed the collected, steadying presence of good leadership better than anyone. He had worked for many large-scale events, including the St. George Hotel fire in downtown Brooklyn a few years before. That incident, with over one-hundred responding apparatus bringing over five-hundred firefighters, involved fire in multiple buildings, narrow streets, and resources from all five-borough as well as an incredible number of relocations to cover neighborhoods devoid of fire coverage.

Relocations are one of the most important roles of a Fire Alarm dispatcher and involve shifting resources from areas where fire response coverage is adequate to areas where coverage is diminished due to various potential reasons, including large scale incidents, multiple companies being out of service, or impending weather conditions such as blizzards or increased risk of brush fires.

When I started, the St. George fire was noteworthy as one of the most significant responses of FDNY apparatus to a structural fire in its history. Between his work experience, his personality, and the support my supervisor showed me, I decided to model myself on him should I ever have the chance to become a supervisor myself. However, through the summer of 2001, I still assumed that would be in some future organization, not the FDNY. The St George fire was not the only incredible event that had been worked by my new coworkers. Many of my colleagues were on duty in 1993 when the previously unthinkable happened. Terrorists attacked the World Trade Center for the first time, employing a truck bomb positioned in one of its parking garages.

Given their experience and their personalities, this core of dispatchers and leaders was far different from any I had encountered in Ohio or anywhere else. Were they all great people? Not exactly. There is a directness found in the fire service world—much more back then than today. Much of our modern interest in creating more agreeable and welcoming working environments was not a concern even as late as 2000 and beyond in the FDNY as well as many other organizations. FDNY was a thoroughly traditional department with an old-school mindset that permeated every aspect of the job. However, just because there was not a conscious effort to be inclusive did not mean the job did not present itself as an opportunity to be somewhere you could belong. Success in belonging was more incumbent on the individual and his or her actions in the process of learning the job. Given my love of community and the fire service, I did my best to fit in as well as I could, to a point. Unfortunately, this point of view was not a universal experience. It would be dishonest not to acknowledge that the department was not then as open as it is today to women and minorities—one of the unfortunate aspects of a more traditional heteronormative organization. Thankfully, this has improved with time and the experiences for all are generally more positive and inclusive today for everyone.

In my service, I passionately committed myself to learning "the job." This included details and information from where the fire companies were located to the response policies, radio procedures, and how to conduct move-ups. I threw myself into the role of being a fire alarm dispatcher. I took it very seriously, even though I still had not committed to the idea of a professional life in the public safety field. Beyond being committed to learning, however, I could be more than a little arrogant and a bit of a know-it-all. I was often asking why things had to be the way they were when, in my mind and vast "multiple month" experience, improvements could be made. Looking back, I wish that I had vocalized less and listened a great deal more, especially to those around me who had worked for some of the busiest years the department had ever known. I missed out on valuable insights because of my approach and those opportunities would soon be gone forever.

However, when I took the time to listen and learn, I found many of the traditions and stability of the organization to be key to its success. That sense of tradition would play a vital role in our ability to meet the challenges of September 11, 2001, and, even more importantly, its aftermath. Despite this, I could have probably been just a little less upfront about my ideas on how to do things better. I could have understood that, for the first year (at least), it is best to learn and observe then figure out how to make changes in those areas where it was most required.

One of the positive side effects of the organization's culture was that it offered a level playing field. The fire department was the fire department. The units were the units, and the decisions to be made during each shift were mostly the same as the day before. However, the timing and geography would change—quickly. Some days, the incidents were spread out over an entire twelve-hour shift, with ample time to grab food or relax between fires. On other days, the activity was constant from when you walked into the building to when you left.

When I arrived as a new fire alarm dispatcher (FAD) at the Brooklyn CO in Group 15 in late December 2000, I was identified frequently by my name, but even more often by my number: Dispatcher 801. The department had started at dispatcher number 101 and moved up from there. Too many dispatchers had been hired and had left in the preceding years. Faced with concern about running out of numbers, my new hire training class was the first issued with temporary numbers, beginning with the number 801. Once we made our year on the job, we were assigned our permanent numbers in the traditional sequence. As the highest civil service ranked dispatcher in my class, I was issued the first number and would be known as Dispatcher 801 on the phones and radio until the closing weeks of 2001.

For the first several months on the floor, I primarily worked on the phones as an ARD. However, as I demonstrated to my supervisor and co-workers that I was proficient in that role, they introduced me to the radio position. FDNY at the time was unique because two dispatchers were assigned to the radio. One person was responsible for speaking over the air with the units in the field, and the other was responsible for managing the CAD screen and entering information coming in from units into a special computer keyboard known as the Status Entry Panel (SEP). This unique way of operating helped ensure that radio transmissions were rarely missed and that the operation could move very quickly, no matter how busy it became.

It is important to note that FDNY's theory of radio operations is much different from most other fire agencies across the United States. It has become commonplace for many agencies in the modern era to have countless channels for units to use. Sometimes, single dispatchers are responsible for monitoring multiple channels simultaneously. This creates confusion as units move between channels and dispatchers miss transmissions or vital information. The FDNY approach was to have all the units in a borough monitor a single frequency at all times for communication with the dispatcher. There are separate radio frequencies for communications between units on the scene, but those are not monitored by fire dispatchers. The fireground frequencies were occasionally supplemented with localized radio repeater systems, such as in high-rise buildings like the World Trade Center. Still, even in those cases, all communications between the dispatcher and every unit in the borough took place on a single radio frequency.

Utilizing this system, the fire dispatcher could be sure of being able to contact any unit over the radio. The unit could be confident that their transmissions would be heard by the dispatcher. The result was a safer, more streamlined operation where everyone in the field and in the central office could maintain a common and coherent operational picture. Yes, it could get hectic, but the ability to maintain control of the units in the field was a critical aspect of the department's effectiveness. Radio transmissions followed clear guidelines, emphasizing the use of codes and language that everyone understood. Units were always to minimize the length of transmissions and effective radio discipline was, and remains, a cultural foundation of the department.

The first nine months of 2001 were all about me learning the job and practicing not just my ability to take calls but also operate the other positions. I also learned as much as possible about the fire department and its operations. I was supported by my supervisor and the team of dispatchers I was a part of. It was a busy summer, with some shifts experiencing five or more working fires in twelve hours. In my five-plus years as a dispatcher in Ohio, I had worked one multiple-alarm fire. In the summer of 2001, there was a shift where we had three—in twelve hours! It was exciting, crazy, and fun.

Things turned a corner financially when I was released for overtime, which I gobbled up with the enthusiasm of a struggling civil service employee from Ohio with an expensive rent bill. My first pay period when I was released for overtime, I managed to clock in ninety-six hours of extra pay. I lived, breathed, and slept at the dispatch office for a month. Still, it was starting to feel like a place I belonged, where I fit in—a job I was coming to see as something I might want to do longer than I planned.

Dispatcher shifts typically began at either 7:00 a.m. or 7:00 p.m. However, you were expected to be at work much earlier as a new dispatcher. We had a policy referred to as early relief, which meant that as soon as someone from the oncoming shift arrived at work and was ready to sit at a position, a person from the off-going shift was permitted to go home. This helped mitigate the long commute times that many dispatchers endured and was a morale booster for everyone. As a probie (probationary dispatcher), however, that privilege was essentially not afforded to you. You were still expected to arrive early so someone else could have the privilege, but you were generally the last person relieved of duty, no matter how early you had reported. It may seem unfair to our present generation, but I typically did not mind it because I was so in love with the work I was doing and wanted to show respect for our senior dispatchers. More time there meant more time for the fires, emergencies, and activity that made the shifts fly by, even when they were extended to eighteen hours due to trades or overtime.

I had not really appreciated how busy some of our days would and could be. The activity level could be intense. Of course, it was not that way all the time, but there were days when we would have ten or more serious fires in a shift just in the borough of Brooklyn. The seven dispatchers and a supervisor were responsible for all the related work, no matter how busy it was. There were no reserve dispatchers in the backroom to call up for help. Because of breaks or people doing administrative work, sometimes you had far fewer people on the operations floor. You truly learned how to do the job efficiently and effectively during these moments. I learned to process inbound 911 calls as soon as I could because the other 911 lines were ringing at the same time and I may be the only call-taker available.

The night of September 10, 2001, was the first of my two-night shifts. I had already arranged a trade for my second night shift (the evening of September 11) because it was my birthday. I told a story about family coming into town to help celebrate, as I needed special permission to arrange a trade. Usually, shift trades (or mutual, as they were called) were not permitted for employees until they had over a year on the job. However, for whatever reason, mine was granted, which meant that after the end of my shift on the night of the tenth, I would have at least five days off work. I had completed my second module of training and was certified to sit at all but one of the dispatcher work positions in the central office. I would not attend Decision Dispatcher school for a while yet, but I was allowed to sit there under some degree of supervision. I had already learned the response policies (what units went on what type of incidents) and understood the geography of Brooklyn and the entire city to some degree. In fact, my love of maps (and my undergraduate geography degree) had come in handy as I developed a goal of knowing the streets of the borough better than most people I worked with.

After all, many New Yorkers are familiar with only their parts of the city (where they live or most often hang out) not the borough or the city as a whole. Overall, I was comfortable and confident in my time in New York City to that point. Although there had been challenges and difficulties, it seemed as though the worst was behind me and that things were actually manageable.

16 | SEPTEMBER 10, 2001

The night shift on September 10 started out quietly. I was working with my usual bunch of co-workers in the Brooklyn CO. September is still warm in New York, and there were the typical crowds of folks hanging around in front of the office and in the nearby park. Our office was in the center of Brooklyn, near Prospect Park and the Brooklyn Botanical Garden, in a neighborhood that had not yet begun to gentrify. In future years, creative real estate agents would try to sell apartments in our area as "Park Slope East," even though we were far more Crown Heights than the swanky other side of Park Slope. Dispatchers learn very early in their careers that weather and co-workers can significantly impact the success (or failure) of their work shifts. However, despite the early calm, the shift would not remain that way.

A water main ruptured just up Washington Avenue from the Brooklyn central office sometime before midnight. The cascade of water flowed into the nearby manhole and, by circumstance, flooded the electrical conduits, knocking out the electricity in a portion of our neighborhood, including our building. Thankfully, the generators kicked on immediately, taking on the load of providing electrical power not just for our lights, but also for all the essential communications systems in the office. They were doing their job through a grinding scream of diesel-generated energy from the basement of our building. Even though shielded under a concrete floor and on the other side of a heavy steel door, the rumble was loud enough to ensure a quiet night was now an impossibility, no matter how many incidents we handled.

The night was made more exciting when one of the department electricians sent to check on the generators realized there was a fuel issue. What followed were a few thrilling moments of bucket brigade diesel deliveries required to ensure we stayed live on our generators until the power was restored. As it often did in late summer, the activity picked up after midnight, with working fires and serious emergencies occurring consistently until it was time for us to head home. It was nothing too crazy, but busy enough between the equipment challenges, the generator, and the activity level that I was exhausted by the time the end of the shift rolled around. It had been so busy that I did not even acknowledge that once the clock had passed midnight, it was my birthday. That celebration would have to wait.

On some mornings, the senior dispatcher and supervisor, who almost always rode to work together, would offer me a ride home. Being in New York City, my usual mode of transport was either the subway or the bus. Knowing how busy our night was, I think they were afraid I might pass out on the subway and end up stuck in the Coney Island yard on an out-of-service train. They offered to give me a ride to my apartment in Sunset Park, about ten minutes out of their way, but that gesture saved me about forty-five minutes of train or bus time. We headed out from the central office through Prospect Park and toward Carroll Gardens, where my supervisor lived with his wife and family in a classic New York City row house apartment. That was our first stop, and then the senior dispatcher and I made our way to Sunset Park, the distinctive Brooklyn neighborhood where I had found my second New York City apartment. I shared the top floor two-bedroom unit with one of those roommates you never really know well but somehow end up living with in big cities with high-housing costs. It's a side effect of New York, I suppose. I cannot even recall how we met and have no idea what became of him. Somehow, we decided to share an apartment, an experiment that would end as soon as the lease did the following June.

By the time I climbed out of the car in front of the building where I lived in that third-floor apartment at the top of creaking, not-so-stable stairs, the sun was painting the streets of Brooklyn in an orange glow. I don't know if the fact that the apartment had been newly renovated after a fire had gutted the entire building added to its mystique or the feeling of structural instability. Still, it was a decent but not spectacular place to live and closer to the city than where I had been in Bay Ridge. So that was a plus.

When I walked up to the door, so tired I struggled to get the key into the lock, not a single cloud was visible in the crystal-clear sky. It looked like the inside of a painting by some French Impressionist who habitually invents the colors he uses because the existing ones just do not do the scene justice. There was no one else on the street around me as I tried to get into the entryway and climb the stairs to the apartment. It was hushed, with little traffic noise, even from the elevated highway at the end of the block.

This ancient block of attached buildings comprised solid rows of multi-family homes, each twenty feet wide, on both sides of 45th Street, running between Third Avenue and Fourth Avenue in the Sunset Park Section of Brooklyn. Sunset Park was an "in-between" neighborhood, trapped in time and space between the rapidly gentrified Park Slope full of queer couples with baby strollers, foie gras, the rolling green of Prospect Park to the north, and the historical permanence of Bay Ridge to the south. To the east was Borough Park, with a southern section of predominantly Asian blocks, and a northern end that featured a Jewish community. Maimonides Hospital at the center of the neighborhood. Sunset Park had a well-lived sheen to it but despite the lack of hipster hangouts, it was a good neighborhood and held onto the feeling of a genuine community, anchored by it largely Spanish speaking population reflected in generations of families who resided there.

Sunset Park did not have the elegance of Park Slope or the charm of Bay Ridge, but it was functional, and a little closer to work and cheaper than my first apartment. The neighborhood was predominantly Latino; many families had settled there decades before and never left. We were all here together, in just a few square miles of land that, in other parts of the US may hold only a handful of residents, who were all largely the same or perhaps even related. In this single block of Brooklyn where I stood on the morning of September 11, 2001, there were probably five hundred people living the day-to-day: fighting the subway, dealing with the lingering summer heat, and connected across boundaries of language, faith, background, or age by the common shared experience of living in New York City. It felt as though none of them were out and about yet. I was alone, pausing, thinking for just a moment about where I had ended up and how I got here.

Sunset Park bordered New York Harbor, with massive dockside concrete structures home to the immense factories that helped America win the Second World War. They now hosted, among many other things, a Costco and a federal prison. Above Third Avenue, between my block and the water, sat the low-seated and hulking steel structure that was the elevated Gowanus Highway. It was a lingering testament to the dream of city planner Robert Moses to crisscross New York City with superhighways, just like in the rest of the county. Its purpose here was to whisk traffic through Brooklyn unmolested by the arduous crawl of the drive through city streets. It sat above the avenues on heavy pillars, which put the highway traffic basically at eye level from the surrounding residents. They lived on upper floors in the houses that sat increasingly higher in elevation as the streets made their way up the low hill on which thew actual City park named Sunset Park sits in a an area bounded 41st and 44th Streets and 5th and 7th Avenues. Whatever its purpose may have been, the reality of traffic and concrete resulted in the Gowanus being just another space for New Yorkers to get stuck in traffic, often more severe than the streets below and far less effective and efficient than subways.

At the other end of my block 45th Street met Fourth Avenue, a broad street built in the spirit of Parisian boulevards but now much more a working-class thoroughfare full of cell phone shops, laundromats, bodegas, and restaurants which alternated between Chinese food (those were often run by Puerto Ricans) and Mexican food (seemingly most often run by Chinese families). Below Fourth Avenue traveled the subway, one of the BMT Lines. BMT stood for Brooklyn Mass Transit back in the day when the New York City subway system was not unified into one publicly managed transit system. History was not past in New York; it was in front of you every day. It was there in the letters of the subway, in the highway that continuously bombed a neighborhood it was supposed to help, and in this row of homes I lived in that had housed countless generations of others trying to make their way forward in this crazy place. The facades changed over time, some suburban-like with vinyl siding and plastic toys in tiny patches of concrete that would be yards in Indiana or Kansas. Because so much of the past was here with you, there was still a feeling of the presence of things and people that came before you. You were always connected to people whose grandchildren died before you were born just because of this particular space. My block did not have the charm of the brownstones or the ivy sandstone of the Upper West Side. Nevertheless, it was as real as all those places and all of those people. You lived in it and around it and it became a part of your skin.

New York City in the early morning is at its most magical, for then and only then, or after a major snowstorm, is it anything close to quiet. All that past, all of those people, even the ominous highway and the distant rumble of the R or N trains are not as present in your view or your thoughts in those rare quiet times. It is not Ohio farmland or Nevada desert quiet. It's just that the noise level is so below where it is during its ordinary daytime course of business that it is striking. You almost feel out of sorts and disoriented, as though your point of reference is missing. Combining the lack of sound with the sky and the orange hue and feeling of peace and place, it was different than any day I had known in New York.

Looking to my right, I could get a solid view of New York Harbor and the blue glass tabletop water at that early hour. It is distinctive how the water looks before being stirred up by all the boats and ships that would later cruise from place to place, carrying people and cargo and all the tourists. Before I stepped inside, in that brief moment of consideration and reflection, maybe subconsciously stirred by it being my birthday, I remember it felt again like home—like someplace I belonged, like I had made the right choice. All the drama, stress, aggravation, the roommates, the move, and the debt all seemed to be worth it. Even though I was utterly exhausted from the night before and maybe everything that had taken place in the entire time I had been in New York, I was in a perfect mood. It was as if I could conquer the world and that New York City would be my place.

Just then, something else caught my eye. Somewhere in New Jersey, off in the distance, an angry, tall column of blackness indicated that on some random street, in some community, a group of firefighters and dispatchers were starting their day with a significant fire. I thought it was probably one of Newark's old warehouses or factories. Odd, I thought, how it keeps going: always fires, emergencies, and always busy.

I silently thanked God I was off for a few days. I went up to the apartment, opened the door, and walked about five feet to my bedroom. It was the smaller of the two. It was actually a glorified closet in classic New York style, only big enough for a twin bed, a clothes rack, and a tiny TV. Thankfully, it at least had a window facing the street. Totally and completely exhausted, I fell onto the bed and passed out, still in my work clothes from the night before—a brilliant combination of extremely happy and completely worn out. I would sleep the sleep of the dead until a little bit after 10:00 a.m. when the unending sounds of sirens, seemingly from everywhere, drove me out of my sleep into a world that had thoroughly and permanently changed in just over two hours. Two hours was how long I got to enjoy the feeling of New York City before it would all change—two hours for which I was not even awake, a span of two hours after which everything that was before would, in many respects, never exist again in the same way.

17 | SEPTEMBER 11, 2001, ABOUT 10:00 A.M.

Sirens are one of New York City's fundamental realities. Fire trucks, ambulances, and police cars are seemingly always in motion, constantly headed to one of the millions of emergencies that occur each year within the city limits. Like those who live near a train track, you eventually acclimate to the noise. It just goes on somewhere in the recesses of your not-so-conscious mind. If it's right in front of you or coming because of an incident you are experiencing, it becomes front of mind, but otherwise, it's not really a big deal.

It was especially odd then to awaken to the sound of sirens. New York City sirens come in as many forms and styles of use as the number of vehicles that utilize them. They can be used just to clear an intersection—the "whoop, whoop" that can often be heard from ambulances. Then there are the fire trucks' passionate, motivated, strong sirens when they are headed to a fire. Those sirens mean business, and you feel compelled to get the hell out of the way and in a hurry. Even on the sidewalk, you move toward the building side and away from the street—just in case.

On the morning of September 11, it was totally different. They were never-ending, a constant barrage of siren screams. There is a type of abnormal sound that, when you hear it, makes you know something is terribly wrong. Parents know it when noisy young children are suddenly silent. A pilot can tell when a certain sound emanates from a sickly aircraft engine. A lover can tell when a question to their beloved is answered with a tone that indicates something IS wrong, even if they say "no."

That was my experience that morning. Something drove me from my sleep and into a seated position on the bed in my tiny bedroom. I put my feet on the floor. My head was still foggy from only two hours of sleep. From where I sat, I reached out and turned on the TV. This was before cable was essential to modern life, much less the streaming, broadband, 500-channel world we find ourselves in today. As we had only recently moved into the apartment and were on a budget, we just had broadcast TV. That meant signals came-in the old-fashioned way: over the airwaves. That also meant that the quality of the TV station signal was determined by the strength of the transmission and its transmitter location. Given that the station I watched most regularly was supported by a tower on the roof of the World Trade Center, there was usually no issue. The picture was always clear and crisp. However, when I turned on the TV, it was clear that something was wrong from the moment the picture came into view. Instead of a clear picture of newscasters telling me the cause of the crescendo of sirens, I was greeted by a screen of grey haze and a slightly mumbled voice. I was disoriented by this, confused really, given that it was so much different than what I had expected to see. The picture was even more grey—the image of smoke. Below that picture, in crawling letters on the bottom of the screen, was the message

WTC Attacked and Destroyed

This was followed shortly by a few more words.

All NYPD and FDNY personnel ordered to return to duty

I realized then that what I heard outside my apartment was the aftermath of the unimaginable. Just a few moments before I turned on the set, the second tower had fallen, and much of Lower Manhattan was now covered in clouds of dust and smoke. I assumed, as did most, that the smoke and the dust were carrying the remains of several thousand people: workers from the towers, bystanders, and, of course, firefighters. I had no idea at that moment the size of the number. However, when you work in public safety for any length of time, you begin to develop an understanding of the unseen and the unstated. Being an effective dispatcher, especially, requires you to be able to construct a view of a scene from minimal information. The few seconds spent with a caller, your knowledge of the geography of your service area, your awareness of fireground operations, and the processes and policies of the fire department mean you can make a good, educated guess about what is going on and what is likely the next step. In this case, seeing the view of what used to be two massive buildings replaced with nothing but suspended ash and the words "attacked" and "destroyed," we knew—all of us knew—the potential scale of the horror. We also knew what we had to do without being told. There was only one place that I belonged. That was at work with my sister and brother members of the New York City Fire Department, doing whatever we could to help mitigate and manage this event and what was potentially to come.

That fire dispatcher-based feeling was professional in its construction. Especially on the worst of the days, you have to fall back into viewing things as a work problem to be solved by a careful systemic application of resources according to established policy, procedure and training. But one of the things that public safety professionals also learn to do because it is essential is turn off the reaction. Subdue the emotional response to the stimuli. That is an essential capability to have any sort of staying power in the profession. If you felt every event or incident, deeply and fully, you would never be able to do the job. On that screen, in the letters scrolling below the image, were words that blew apart, just for an instant, that system of checks and balances that all of us leverage to do our jobs, day in and day out. It was a sucker-punch to the soul and, more importantly, the process. A scale of impact so far beyond what we plan for, and develop tricks to manage, that it actually took my breath away for more than a moment. I had to find that strength again if I was going to go to work and be of any functional use to the city, its Fire Department, and my fellow dispatchers.

At that moment, my mind raced back to the drills we had recently had. There were conversations in the office about what to do in the event of a terror attack on New York City. We had talked as a group in the office a few times about the 1993 bombing and how the efforts had been to get the world's attention focused on New York City. After all, all the media was here. The financial hub of the world was here. Tourists from all over the world were here. New York City was and remains one of the greatest opportunities for terrorists to gain attention in the entire world. On the morning of 9/11, my first thought as I worked to muster together my plan about what to do next was to acknowledge that this may be only the beginning. It dawned on me that this could be an opening act to bring a later, even more horrific event upon the world via New York City. I would find out later that I was not the only person to have that thought that day. What happened next occurred despite that thought—or maybe even because of it. We all went to work anyway.

Whether a firefighter, dispatcher, emergency medical technician, or police officer, we went. Everyone I knew, whatever his or her role, found a way to move beyond the fear of knowing that this could be the beginning of an end and went to work. Largely ignored was the reality of the operational danger or the potential that New York City was about to be nuked or hit with some sort of biological attack that would kill us all. We went to be a part of the bigger thing: the response, the help. It may have been the only thing we could have done. It may have been the opposite of what non-public safety folks would do, but that is not entirely true. The stories of New Yorkers helping New Yorkers became legendary and would fill the pages of the newspapers for weeks. People dropped what they were doing without prompting, without examination of background or papers, religious or political affiliation. They became a part of the response, some in a very small local way, some in ways that helped to save countless lives. They became focused, despite the incredible fear that permeated the entire region, on saving lives and helping strangers. Although we in public safety perhaps felt it more directly in some ways, so many saw the planes hit, towers fall, and smoke and ash rise. This was a global shock that radiated across those in New York and surrounding areas in ways that had never ever occurred before. Never before had an event like this happened on live television broadcast globally. Yes, there had been tragedies before, like the Space Shuttle Challenger. And there had been attacks. But December 7th, 1941 was mostly read about in newspapers the day after or heard about on the radio. For those present it was an entirely different experience altogether and that was the reality for the millions who saw the smoke and who felt the events of September 11th, 2001 in the deepest recesses of themselves. And yet, they would find a path forward and help.

Somewhere, somehow, I found that strength to center my thoughts and to start heading to work. My next step was to begin to pack. I suspected I would be at work for two or three days and knew I needed to be prepared. I threw some basic clothes and a shaving kit into a bag. Then I grabbed a quick shower, thinking I would need it to at least wake myself up and focus on what I needed to do. Before leaving the apartment to head to work, I tried to make the call. The call is that one call you make when you are unsure whether you will get another for a while or ever. I wanted to speak to my parents, to let them know I was okay, and that I would be back in touch as soon as I could. I made multiple attempts, but it was not meant to be. The telephone circuits were simply too jammed to allow me to make this one request. I would try again, I told myself. Then, I headed down the apartment stairs to the street, evaluating what the best way would be to make my way to our Brooklyn central office.

I opened the door into some sort of alternate Land of Oz. Like Dorothy, I had been asleep and terrified and shaken awake by events far beyond my control. And, like Dorothy, I opened a door with hesitation and fear, sensing what was on the other side would be different—unimaginably different. I had no choice. I had to go and face what was outside. I stepped out onto the sidewalk and took a few steps, pausing just a few feet from the front door of the building. It was then that I looked up.

I saw the face of death or Satan or evil, or whatever describes the most terrifying thing you may ever see in your life: swirling, black, acrid clouds a few hundred feet above my head, twisting with power and rage. It took my breath away. In my time associated with the fire service in one capacity or another, I have been to probably a thousand fires, maybe more. I have been to fires in factories, homes, vehicles, and countless other places. Nothing that I had ever seen, or would ever see, would compare to the image of that raging cloud against that morning sky. Knowing just a little bit about fires made it all the worse because you knew what was in that cloud and what had to happen to cause a cloud of smoke to move like that and have that color. The smoke, created by fires after all, is the byproduct of whatever is burning. This was the byproduct of an unimaginable number of physical things, from building materials to office chairs and electrical systems to the debris from the aircraft that had hit the towers. It was also the remains of the people who had been lost. That insane witch's brew created something that defied explanation until you stopped to actually consider just how much stuff was being consumed with just how much heat and what the effect of that could be. It towered over the city and streaked to the south and southeast with such ferocity it carried larger items with it, much like a tornado on the American Plains. This darkness was not harmless farmland dirt being carried aloft, but things much more precious and human.

Once I regained my breath, I walked up 45th Street toward Fourth Avenue. My first choice of how to get to work was to take the R or N train from 45th Street to Atlantic Avenue, where I would cross over to take a Coney Island-bound train to the Empire Boulevard stop across the street from our office. It became immediately apparent that the train would not be an option, though, as all services had been suspended. I would find out later that the damage to the subway system from the falling towers had been significant. Plan B was to think about the bus, but the traffic had already become intense, making the bus idea a nonstarter. At that moment, standing at the corner of 45th Street and Fourth Avenue, I caught sight of a fire engine a few blocks north. It was one of our special reserve engines, only utilized for disasters when off-duty personnel were recalled to cover empty firehouses. I was amazed these were already on the street, but then the site of that ancient engine pressed into service reminded me again of just how real this event was. Somewhere in the deepest recesses of my mind, I think I may have held out hope this was just a crazy dream, but that early 1980s Mack CF pumper chugging down Fourth Avenue put the final nail in the coffin of anything but firm resolution that this was not a dream—there would be no Dorothy-like happy ending.

As if that was not enough, this was also the moment when I noticed the people around me. They were slowly, silently walking down the sidewalk on Fourth Avenue. Looking at them, they reminded me of elementary school kids on a field trip—the well-behaved kind who made the presence of a gaggle of monitors redundant. These kids would not be giving anyone any trouble. They were so silent, almost no speaking between them, as if they were too stunned by the events of the day to have anything to add to it. Some were also covered in ash, dirt, and debris. They were, as I realized, trying to make their way home from Lower Manhattan. It was obvious some had walked the entire way, escaping hell over the classic suspended walkways of the Brooklyn Bridge. Others had likely tried to make it home by subway or bus, only to be ejected onto the street to make their own way once those services were shut down in the interest of safety. Here they now were, walking two by two, toward home in one sense, but toward the unknown in another. In some ways they looked like silent zombies, trying to find the most important thing they could in the face of the terror they lived that morning—this crowd of silent, stunned, ashen people. To be sure, they were still New Yorkers. Some moved more quickly and assuredly, as though there were loved ones a few blocks away they had to get to. Others walked at a much slower pace, as if unsure of where their next step would take them.

New Yorkers pride themselves on always having an answer—always having an angle. They may not be able to tell you the names of all fifty states, or even more than five, but they know how to navigate their own worlds with the talent of a Steph Curry or a Rembrandt. They can figure out how to get a cab to take them from Manhattan to Brooklyn, when the best time to get to the deli is, and how to navigate the crushing crowds of Times Square (they never go in the first place). They can wake up on the subway five seconds before their stop. They can win a fistfight with a bar buddy over the Jets versus the Giants and then turn around and buy that same, now slightly bloody and bruised, buddy a beer. To watch them work in their natural habitat is a gift. That morning, it was all broken. To see all that self-assuredness, confidence, and peace of mind wiped away in the stone-grey covered faces of those people was to see a world removed and replaced with something different, something unfamiliar—and the day was just beginning.

Faced with no mass-transit option to get to work, I went to the next best thing: the local livery cab service. In New York City, there were, at the time, two types of cabs. One type was the ubiquitous yellow cabs, which you could hail on the street. The other, less well-known type was livery cabs, or car services. Almost always black in color, these cabs were either requested by phone or you could walk to their dispatch office and request a ride. They were a little nicer than the yellow cabs and a bit more expensive in some instances. I walked into the dispatch office of our neighborhood livery cab service on 45th Street just east of 4th Avenue. I forcefully shared that I was a fire department employee who needed to get to Empire and Washington Avenues in Brooklyn. I showed my FDNY ID. The dispatcher immediately, without even a question, set about finding me a car. After a moment or two, he leaned out and asked a question. He had several other passengers who needed to get to that same part of Brooklyn. He asked if I would be willing to share my ride with them. Going with me would ensure they could get there, because having an FDNY member in the car meant getting through any roadblocks that may have been created to secure certain areas or improve traffic flow. I offered no resistance to that plan, and when the car arrived a little while later, we all piled in and started on the journey to the east side of Prospect Park. Usually, this would be about a ten-minute ride, but that morning, owing to the traffic and the multitudes of people on the street, I remember it taking much longer. The journey was narrated by an AM news radio station offering continuous updates of the day's events. There were reports of attacks in Washington, DC (true), a mysterious plane crash in Pennsylvania that may have been related (also true), and myriad other happenings in New York City that, to the best of my knowledge, were unfounded. It felt like a slow drive to the end of the world, accompanied by strangers. Our destination known but unknown and making such insanely slow progress. I am still struck by how quiet it was. Just like the people on the street, our small band of passengers was eerily silent—pushed to a terrified silence by the events of the day and the fear of what was going to happen next.

18 | THE BROOKLYN CENTRAL OFFICE ON SEPTEMBER 11, 2001

We finally got close to the fire department central office after untold minutes in the car—probably an hour journey or more. The street in front of the office was closed, with barricading fire department vehicles providing some sense of security. I do not recall seeing a single police officer anywhere in the area, only FDNY department personnel from our communications bureau. I made my way to the front door of our building, pounded on the door, and rang the bell. A dispatcher who had started on the job in the class before mine answered the door. I walked into the office, into a determined and crazed atmosphere of "we have a job to do" but also into the unspoken shock surrounding what that job actually was and would continue to be, but gratefully no longer alone.

I walked across the floor to sign in to the journal book. As I looked around the room, I took a brief look at who was in the building. There was the on-duty shift, and most of my regular co-workers were also there. A colleague said, "This came from our parking lot." I looked down and took it into my hand for a quick review. It was labeled "Cantor Fitzgerald." I think it was a ledger sheet of some type, but about half the page was gone, and a black sear ran across the edge of what remained. This was a chilling statement about just what had occurred to bring a simple piece of paper about five miles from Manhattan to Brooklyn. That same smoke I had seen when leaving my apartment was full of this kind of stuff. But it was not just stuff. It was a piece of work created by a person at a company in a building of which every element was now gone. That paper also suggested, in no uncertain terms, the incredible number of other people, other companies, and other ways this event had impacted everyone. Like when I saw the TV screen a few hours before, it took my breath away for a moment and forced me to refocus on the task at hand while considering just what had occurred.

Everything that had happened meant the day shift working across all five offices had processed hundreds of calls for assistance from people in the towers. The vast majority of those callers did not survive. It meant that the dispatchers had coordinated the response of hundreds of FDNY fire companies to that same incident and now many of those same firefighters were buried under countless tons of rubble. It meant that this group of professionals, assisted by their colleagues now streaming into the Central Offices of each of the five boroughs, would have to develop and implement a path forward to ensure that whatever came next would be able to be managed not just today, but also in the days to come.

One of the aspects of that day that few seem to remember was that the collapse of the Twin Towers was not the end of the event by any means. Even though the two most significant buildings were now piles of burning debris, other buildings were still on fire in Lower Manhattan. The aircraft debris and the Towers' collapse caused significant damage to many different structures. Many of those structures, as well as the towers, had been occupied, and now rescue efforts were underway to attempt to dig out those who had been buried or who were trapped in other related emergency situations. The Towers' collapse also crushed the underground structures below and near the World Trade Center site and elements of the water supply system. This included several subway and transit lines, an underground mall, and multiple other facilities. There was also the challenge of getting injured people to hospitals and ensuring that the FDNY could still respond to other emergencies and fires elsewhere in New York City. Any city, and especially one the size of New York, does not stop just because of one epic disaster, and ensuring the FDNY's ability to keep the overall operation going no matter how horrified we all were was not a function we could forget about just because we were in the midst of a massive terrorist attack.

Although our mission to coordinate the response to the Towers and other emergencies was clear, how to accomplish that mission was not. Our fire department was largely gone, either buried under the rubble and lost, buried and in the process of being rescued, or missing the apparatus and equipment required to do their job. An enormous number of personnel and apparatus had been dispatched to Lower Manhattan, and now many of those resources would be unavailable to us for a very long time. Even more significantly, many of the personnel now feared lost in the rubble were the decision makers and leaders of the fire department, just the kinds of people who would be tasked with figuring out how to manage this type of event. We had received word from those at the scene that the first deputy fire commissioner, chief of the fire department, and so many others, were dead. It was like one of those Civil War battles where the generals went down, and then the colonels, and some lower-level officers were forced to rise above their ranks, or else all would be lost. It was the ultimate repudiation of the flippant phrase too often uttered in response to workplace challenges: "That's above my pay grade." Even thinking that on this day would have been a crime.

On that day, in that situation, a combination of the dispatch command and supervision staff along with selected members of the FDNY chief ranks remained. They organized the operation to provide resources not just for the rescue operation at the Towers, but for the response to other fires and emergencies in New York City. For the first time, a coordinated mutual-aid request was made to surrounding counties and states for apparatus to respond into the city of New York. Some of these resources came on their own. However, this small group of leaders, realizing we were facing a challenge that would be insurmountable without help, planned the majority of requests. This would be especially true should an additional attack happen on the city, something we all feared, if only in the deepest recesses of our minds.

Mutual aid fire companies from New Jersey would respond in Staten Island and Brooklyn. Mutual aid from Long Island would respond to Queens. Mutual aid from Westchester County and beyond would respond initially to the Bronx. To what extent mutual aid made it to Manhattan firehouses remains unclear to this day, partly because of the segmented nature of how the mutual aid was handled. However, in Brooklyn, we mustered approximately twenty mutual aid engine companies and fifteen mutual aid ladder companies to cover Brooklyn firehouses.

At some point in that process, I was assigned my first formal task of the day, owing to the relatively decent handwriting for which I had a reputation. I was asked to take a legal pad and write on one sheet where the mutual aid engines were to be sent, how we would designate them in our CAD system for tracking, and on another sheet to do the same for the ladder companies. I then took the sheets, photocopied them, placed them at all the positions, and ensured the dispatchers knew they were there.

A little while after completing that assignment, I was directed to the radio position, where I would be the voice of Brooklyn fire dispatch for the next ten or so hours. Around the same time, I noticed for the first time the distinct ring of our private phone. By contract, dispatchers were provided with one unrecorded phone line in each of our offices for personal phone calls. Cell phones at the time were around, of course, but not anywhere near today's level of use. As this phone was answered and the dispatcher in our office listened to the voice on the other end, a gut-wrenching pattern began—a phone call to give us a heads-up about someone who had been lost. In this case, the first call I received was one to share the death of Captain Timothy Stackpole, an FDNY member who had only recently returned to duty after being severely burned in a spectacular multi-alarm fire and collapse in Brooklyn three years before. Two firefighters from Brooklyn had been lost in that earlier fire and Captain Stackpole had barely survived. The dispatcher accepted the news, choked down into her gut the start of a wail, hung up, shared the news with the office, and then continued on with her duties, just like the rest of us. The cycle of ringing, a face momentarily crushed with sadness, and then a perfunctory announcement would be shared over and over again that day. It became something like a routine. The only more dramatic moments were when individuals who had been at the World Trade Center arrived at our building after finding their way through the aftermath "home" to the central office. They all arrived in much the same form. They were in shock, covered in ash and dust, and mostly unable to describe what they had experienced. How could they? It was so beyond anything that they or anyone else could have imagined. Each of these arrivals required acknowledgement from those working on the floor in the way I imagine soldiers act when a comrade missing from a crazed battlefield retreat is located. There was a moment of two of recap: What had you seen? Did anyone else not make it? There was precious little celebration because it was part of something much more complex that was still ongoing.

Throughout those hours, our office served as a collection point. A Noah's Ark where we rode out a disaster that would change the course of our earth by collecting survivors in ones, twos, and threes, and gathering information and updates about the human cost of the catastrophe as well as operational guidance on how we were going to move forward. The phone rang frequently with calls from firehouses and off-duty members as well. As the firefighters who were off duty made it back to their home quarters they desperately wanted to help. Mostly they wanted to respond to the towers to help in the rescue of their fellow firefighters who were buried under the rubble. In place of being able to do that, which was restricted quite early, they wanted to do what they knew how to do—they wanted to respond to fires. But there were only so many reserve apparatus for them to use. It became a sort of game for them to find any vehicle they could throw their equipment onto and respond to incidents with apparatus which was not normally used for fires was pressed into service, with members riding on any seat or bench they could find to help cover the city for other events. Older fire trucks and those needing repair were scavenged back into service. All while operations at the Towers themselves continued and every member of the FDNY awaited more information about the human toll on civilians and members of the department

It has become almost a cliché that there are funny or at least heartwarming moments in disasters as well. That was true for this day, too, and it took the form of a co-worker who had always been a challenging teammate. To say he was not exceptionally skilled at his job would be kind, but I had always gotten along with him well. He had a reputation for avoiding work on the busiest parts of shifts or during periods when we had a reasonable guess it would be active. On September 11th he had been in the CO for the day tour, coming in that morning as I was leaving. At some point, amid the ringing phones and never-ending radio traffic, someone realized that this individual was not to be found on the operations floor. By then, dozens of other personnel were in the building, so no call, radio transmission, or other task was left undone or unanswered because of his absence. It was just odd that he was missing. In fact, he had left the building, and no one knew where he had gone.

A swift and efficient "on the job" justice system adjudicates actions unbecoming during times of crisis. You are immediately tried by your peers and convicted. The subsequent discussion centers around the various punishments available: "We will never work a mutual (trade) for that guy again" or "Let's see if he ever gets called for overtime." Owing to the activity level that day, the sentencing phase of the trial was very short, and everyone moved on about their tasks. In some ways, it gave us hope that even amid such chaos, some things remained the same, even the perceived laziness and lack of dedication of our co-workers.

At that moment, the office's front door opened, and a small bucket brigade began to form. I had gotten up to get something to drink and witnessed a sight that defied both expectation and easy explanation. The bucket brigade was formed from the back of our missing co-worker's Suburban, now parked on the street in front of the office, into our building's kitchen. People were passing along box after box of food—huge boxes that were very full. After everything was put away or at least in one area, our miscreant dispatcher announced to the jury of his peers that a deli-owning friend from Bensonhurst in Brooklyn had offered all the food he had in the shop for the dispatchers in the Brooklyn CO if transportation could be arranged. Our co-worker was more than happy to go retrieve the donation and made a point to add that he knew he would not be missed anyway. He had done the one thing he knew he could do to help. It is just like a dispatcher to not only solve a problem and go out of his way to do so but be pithy about it in the process.

With the combination of the donation and a biblical scale feast of food prepared from the leftovers in the Brooklyn Central Office kitchen by another industrious co-worker using leftovers and standard cupboard items, we settled in for what continued to be an intense day.

As the shift on September 11th progressed, the disaster in lower Manhattan continued, including the fires that burned long after the towers had collapsed. One of those subsequent fires led to the eventual collapse of Seven World Trade in the late afternoon. This event was shared on our Brooklyn radio frequency by the fireboats deployed to supplant the damaged water system of Lower Manhattan to provide water for firefighting. This occurred while FDNY Dispatchers, including those of us in Brooklyn, engaged in the never-before-witnessed task of coordinating the response of mutual aid units to fires and emergencies. Given the inability of mutual aid units to speak to us and be assigned incidents on the borough radio frequencies, we designed a system of task forces. One FDNY unit would be paired with two mutual aid units, with one member of the

FDNY on each of the mutual aid rigs equipped with a portable radio and tasked with being the communications relay point between the fire trucks in the task force and the Dispatch Central Office. This way we would be able to relay critical information and geographic instructions as well as the incidents to which the task forces were dispatched. This was long before GPS-enabled mobile phones or computer provided turn-by-turn directions. The mutual aid units were largely unfamiliar with every aspect of FDNY operations and New York City geography. The system worked as long as the companies stayed together, but they required frequent reminders to maintain this foreign way of operating. Providing these reminders was one of my primary jobs at the Radio Dispatch position in Brooklyn, where I had been assigned since early in the afternoon.

In time, additional FDNY units began to come into service. Using spare apparatus (which is not generally equipped for operations), remaining reserve apparatus and support vehicles repurposed into fire apparatus, we began to create a fire department able to operate in a rudimentary but somewhat effective manner. In the same space, there was gratitude for the mutual aid companies but also a feeling that FDNY wanted to protect New York. The goal was to reduce our need for mutual aid as quickly and effectively as possible.

Through it all, we began to realize something strange about the day. Other than the events in Lower Manhattan, the rest of the city was middle of the night quiet, despite it being our normal peak time of activity. Only one other working fire occurred in those twenty-four hours, whereas there would be nine or ten in an average period. It seemed there were fewer emergencies, too, from stuck elevators to auto accidents. It was as though the entire city had stopped in its tracks and held its breath as it worked through the calamity that was befalling New York and our nation.

It also became clear over time how big of a disaster it was. An odd sort of equation would play out over the coming days. The number of civilians who had been lost in the Towers was reduced from early estimates of up to 10,000. However, our departmental assumptions about the human and departmental cost of saving those lives had been increasingly validated and escalated. As more and more phone calls came in, we learned of more and more firefighters who had paid the ultimate price. The names came in torrents at times. Entire crews were lost, especially our elite special operations units, the go-to responders for complex fires and emergencies. We knew many of them personally. Just a month or two before, I had spent time talking with the captain of Rescue Company One, Terry Hatton, and several members of his company while I was working in the Manhattan central office on a detail. They were being followed by a camera crew. I think every member I chatted with that night was lost, along with so many others who often visited our central offices. These were personnel I had ridden with, folks who we went to parties with, who we hosted fundraisers for, and who were a part of our family.

The management of the actual event continued to occur in concert with our increasing awareness of how badly our human losses were. The news came about Father Mychal Judge, the legendary FDNY chaplain who served as spiritual advisor for the department and his parish. He was one of the first announced casualties from the collapse, with the photo of his body being carried from the pile of debris serving as one of the most powerful images of that morning. The losses of the longtime FDNY First Deputy Commissioner William Feehan and the Chief of Department Peter Ganci Jr. were officially confirmed as well as other chiefs and department leaders. We found out about entire companies of firefighters that had been lost—such as Rescue Company One and their legendary leader Terry Hatton, along with Ladder Company Three and their own incredible Captain Patrick Brown.

We also learned just how close dispatchers had come to being casualties. The field communications unit, an FDNY team that responds to major incidents to provide on-scene communications support, had responded early on to the Towers. It was relatively close when the buildings collapsed. An I-beam landed directly on the top of the rig. The members would likely have been crushed if they had been in their regular apparatus. Instead, as they were in a spare rig with entry doors on the rear of the truck rather than on the side, they were blown out of the back of the unit onto the street and survived.

All through the afternoon, these reports continued, with scattered samples of survival stories sometimes shared with hopeful statements about the rescue mission underway to find anyone who could have survived the towers' collapse. There would be very few successful conclusions of those stories in the coming days. In truth, as we all knew, survival in or under a collapsed complex of buildings of that size was extremely unlikely. We knew that what was really underway was a recovery operation, not just of those we had lost and the civilians who had been in the Towers that morning, but of our department, our city, and, in many ways, ourselves.

At midnight that night, with relatively little activity occurring other than at Ground Zero, most of the additional personnel who had reported to duty were sent home. We had all been relatively isolated while we were at work, focused on the mission at hand. There was little time to watch news coverage or digest any of what had happened while we were in the middle of it. In fact, I think we all would have stayed for weeks had we been allowed. However, the bosses knew there would be more to do in the coming days, so we were given the order to head home. We heard that of our two hundred or so fire dispatch personnel, only four had not made it into one of our central offices on that day to help in whatever way they could. Those who did not make it were on a road trip together, one that they ended early so they could drive straight through back to the East Coast, arriving in New York City a couple of days later.

19 | THE AFTER

When I was relieved of duty that night, just like after the previous shift, a dispatcher with a few more years on the job offered me a ride home. I asked him not to take me home, though. I just did not want to be alone. Not after that day—not after what had happened. Going home to sit in that lonely, tiny apartment, in that cell of a bedroom or with a roommate I did not even like felt as if it was the worst possible thing to do. I had my co-worker drop me off at one of my favorite bars in Park Slope. A lesbian bar primarily, it was open to anyone, and I was "bar acquaintances" with the bartender. I made my way in and was surprised to see no one else in the bar except the bartender. I think he was there because he, too, knew of nowhere else he would want to be, even if no one else was there. We did not talk much about anything at all. It was just a place to be in silent companionship in the after effect of a horrible event that defied easy discussion.

    I sat at the bar, ordered a White Russian, and just silently reflected. The day's experiences poured over me, but I did not feel like sharing them or even saying them out loud. I just knew I did not want or need to be alone. I guess it's a rare thing to want to be around other people but not want to speak. Maybe it's a consequence of not knowing what to say, fear of someone else saying the wrong thing, or maybe being terrified of falling apart from the inside if you open your mouth. Eventually, a couple of other patrons came in, acting like people with no concept of the severity of the events of that day. To escape their attempt to chat with me no matter how little returning interest I showed, I walked across the street to another bar and found the safety of the corner stool nestled up against the wall with a view of the entire place before me. I still did not want to chat, but I still did not want to be alone. That bartender, too, knew me, and he brought over my White Russian and rubbed my back, much like the bartender of a couple of years before with whom I had sought comfort on another horrible day of a much different kind. It is a truth of my life that museums, churches, bars, and diners have always been, and will always be, my refuge. Strange how some of the closest people to us are not friends exactly. They may know what you need most in a moment but nothing at all about your whole self, only your first name, your favorite dinner order, or your drink of choice. Communities are strange that way, and familiarity can come in many different forms. Put another way, angels appear in mysterious ways.

Unfortunately, the two chatty patrons from the other bar followed me across the street and made some comments that were—unsupportive. It was the oddest thing to be dealing with people who seemed so disconnected from what everyone else in New York City—no, the world—was feeling at that moment. As I got up to start some sort of confrontation and share the feelings that had been welling inside me for hours now with no release, the strangest thing happened: my cell phone rang. It was someone I knew from Pennsylvania calling to check on me.

I told him to hold on, paid my bar tab, and then walked home to Sunset Park, about forty blocks from where I was. I do not remember anything about the conversation. I do not even remember the name of the person who called me. But I do know that the voice of someone who cared enough to call—that ringing phone on that night of all nights—brought me back to life at least a little bit, enough to re-center myself. Combined with the kindness of my bartenders and the inspiring work of my fellow dispatchers that day, it provided some sense of how to move forward.

20 | SEPTEMBER 12 AND BEYOND

The next six months of working in the FDNY became a blur. There were constantly new policies and procedures to follow. The department was finding its way forward, facing the increasing reality of what it had lost. Our special operations units were reduced to minimal use as the department tried to reconstitute the companies that had been decimated in apparatus and their members. Three-hundred-forty-three would be the final tally of members lost. A number that will be etched permanently on the history of FDNY. It would appear on signs and patches and even be the name of a new fireboat placed in service years later. It would be the largest loss of firefighters in history from a single event anywhere and echo in ways that the department still reflects to this day. For everyone in the department no matter what their role, the day would serve as inspiration and motivation but also mission. Returning to something more normal would take a very long time. The smoke from the Towers would continue to spiral over the city for weeks after.

Even in the shadow of that smoke, the rest of the city continued on, slowly stirring back to something like routine life as the impacts from that day simultaneously became more understood and more manageable. Photos of missing loved ones began to appear, most prominently at Union Square Park in Manhattan. Stories circulated of the last phone calls, the narrow escapes, the circumstances that led people to a horrible fate in Lower Manhattan on that day or away from it.

MIRACLES & MILESTONES

The Fire Department also started to implement one of the most solemn traditions in its legacy of honoring those who gave the ultimate measure of devotion. It began announcing to the department the names of the members who had been lost, known to those familiar as announcing the "four fives." This was something a dispatcher would likely do only a few times in a career. For those on the job those weeks in September of 2001, it became almost routine. Some days, we would read one at a time. One day, later in the week, I believe we read sixteen in one batch. Finally, at some point, the decision was made that we would reserve all the announcements and do them in one large batch on the first anniversary. For September 11, 2001, the reading of the "four fives" became more like a sledgehammer reminder of where we were, what had happened, and the extent to which things would never be the same—even though all the announcements themselves were very much the same.

It is with regret that the department announces the death of firefighter (insert name) which occurred on September 11th, 2001, as a result of injuries sustained while operating at Manhattan 5th Alarm Box 8087, transmitted at 08:47 hours. Signed ____.

Beyond the work lives that all of us were trying to navigate, there were the home lives as well. It is an odd testament to the nature of those who worked in the fire department that I do not recall anyone losing a family member in the attacks other than firefighters or police officers. The public safety forces of the city of New York are in many ways segregated from the parts of New York that so many imagine as being "real." We were largely disconnected from the stockbrokers, Wall Street executives, consultants, and other white-collar workers whose offices were located in the Towers. New York is also separated by geography. With many members of FDNY and NYPD living in areas on the outskirts of the city or even on Long Island or upstate, there was a striking distance between the people who protected the city and the people who needed protecting. It became clear on 9/11, and even more so in the subsequent days, that the perceived distance between those two groups was at least temporarily eliminated, as it was to some degree between all New Yorkers.

As it became clear that 343 FDNY members had been lost in the process of saving more than ten thousand civilians from the towers, there was a palpable feeling of gratitude and respect that developed in the city. That feeling swelled outward until it turned New York into the largest small town in the world. It was as though everyone was grateful to still be alive and, at least in some small way, in need of connection to their neighbors. The number of people who brought food, flowers, and other tokens of appreciation to their local firehouses was exceeded only by the number of people who did small, random, forever unknown acts of kindness for their neighbors. Scientists may scoff at the assertion (I do not know if there is data to back it up) that, in the face of the trauma of that day, the city felt differently, and it acted differently. It begs the question of how the aftermath of a similar event would be different today in our much more polarized world, but I hope it would be the same. I hope that millions of people, facing the unthinkable but having witnessed inspired acts of humanity and heroism, would feel called not to engage in social media diatribes or torch-lit mob marches of hatred but follow the same path of community and connectedness that marked the days after 9/11.

As the weeks and months progressed, things began to navigate back toward normal. Our work environment settled in, the subway system was somewhat restored to normal operations, and the parade of well-wishers dropping off food trickled down to zero. However, there was never a single moment of reckoning for what we had experienced. There was no big post-incident debrief for those who worked the event and its aftermath. Indeed, some stories were shared, but in the oldest of old-school traditions, there was a sense that the best way to recover was just to move on and keep getting the job done. That continued through all the funerals, all the memorials, and the reality that the rescue effort turned into recovery operations. The incident itself continued for longer than many outside of New York realized. Challenged by the sheer magnitude of the debris pile and the goal of recovering the remains of those caught in the collapse, the fires consuming what were the Towers would continue to burn for one hundred days. What debris was not consumed by fire would remain for far longer. One of the buildings severely damaged by aircraft parts flying off the Towers, the Deutsche Bank Building, would become its own historic incident six years later. Even in August of 2025, victims were being identified through DNA testing of human remains. Eleven thousand members of the FDNY, NYPD, and other public safety groups are suffering today from the health impacts, including over 3,500 battling cancer. This clearly illustrates just how much September 11, 2001, remains not an event of the past, but of the present.

In the immediate aftermath, before these facts were known, the department and the city tried their best to move on. One critical piece of moving on somehow became the first trip a few co-workers and I made to Ground Zero. Although we knew very well what had happened there and had a notion of what to expect courtesy of news reports, videos, and the many co-workers who had been to the site, there was nothing that could prepare you for the experience of walking the streets of Lower Manhattan around the site where the Towers had stood.

As someone passionate about urban geography, I am almost always viewing things through scales: the scale of what one-inch equals on a map, or the scale of what it is like as a human being to stand on a street that was either designed for humans and horses in the 1800s or cars and trucks and all things "modern" in the 1950s. The ability of a place to create a feeling (good, bad, or indifferent, or even all three simultaneously) is one of the most remarkable aspects about how we interact with our surroundings. The Towers and their surrounding plazas were never the warmest of places. They could be barren, especially on cloudy days, as their features pronounced a time of industry, success, and progress. But in the aftermath of 9/11, this part of New York City was a place that generated the strongest feelings possible.

Here we now were, slowly walking the canyon streets, closer and closer to the pile of debris, fire, sadness, and rage that was just a few weeks before one of the world's most outstanding architectural achievements. The smoke oozed out and around the buildings. The sounds of recovery and removal were familiar, like those at a giant construction site. But knowing what had happened here made that feeling something strange. This was not construction or creation, this was a testament to destruction, fear, and terror. The surreal was everywhere and forced the question of what really is surreal in an environment where everything is. On certain blocks, there were oddly forgotten cars—left behind in the clean-up for some unknown reason, perhaps because their owners did not survive to recover them. Building after building was damaged, boarded up, and seemingly abandoned. Long before you got close to the site, you could see glimpses of what had been left of the buildings of the World Trade Center. Blackened, charred, and battered shards of steel and concrete were left to sprout up from the ground. They were like Nebraska corn stalks, perverted in the place, purpose, and source. The smoke rose up behind them and over them. No longer did the smoke push with the horrible, intense anger of those first days. Now it seeped from somewhere deep within the pile, giving the impression that it would never be able to be extinguished.

The people scurried about in their modes of recovery, focused on doing what they could to bring order to the aftermath, even though at first and second appearance, it was almost comical to think that anything could bring order to the indescribable ruins before us. Two of the most significant buildings ever constructed by humankind were now in piles. Many other buildings met the same fate and were in connected, interrelated heaps around the collapsed towers themselves. It was as though the angriest toddler ever had run amuck across the landscape of Lower Manhattan, not caring a bit about the consequences. Amid this visual chaos, there was another component: the combined burning smell of the debris and human remains of those who had found their final resting place somewhere in that Tuesday morning hellscape. Many would never be found.

Ashes to ashes and dust to dust, from dust you came and to dust you will return.

Between the sights, the smells, and the awareness of the scale of the destruction, it was too much. For each of us, there is a breaking point beyond which we can no longer effectively operate. Sometimes, we realize too late where the border lies between the version of ourselves that can function effectively in the world and the "other" us. The version that would hide under the bed or in the closet, waiting for the inevitable end, less afraid of our inevitable end than anything else that could happen on the way there. You are changed forever once you peer over the side of those cliff walls. That was the view on the streets of Lower Manhattan, looking at what was and knowing that things would never be the same. Yes, they would rebuild. Of course, they would rebuild. Our national psyche, ego, and pride could never allow anything except something even more grand to occupy a space of such tragedy and horror. However, those new buildings would be years away. Even thoroughly clearing the site and fully recovering the remains of those who could be recovered was years away. In the shadow of what remained, what had been lost was crystal clear: not just a building but so much more. That made it too much to bear.

I would not return to the site for a very long time; it was just too hard. Everything about my move to New York City was reflected in the World Trade Center site. I had been on the rooftop observation deck in 1995. I enjoyed attending events on the plaza and hanging out in the stores. I passed under them on the subway many of the times I had gone into Manhattan and, of course, they were in view any time you gazed at the skyline. I was still new enough to New York then that the places occupied an outsized position in my feelings about my new hometown. I did not have a giant core of people to be my network yet. So the spaces I frequented took on that role. The Grand Central Terminal; Central Park; The Subway; the 69th Street Pier in Brooklyn, and The World Trade Center. My geography interest further enhanced my connections to these amazing places and now, one the most prominent was gone. Not because of some natural disaster but because of the anger and hate in the world that had expressed itself in a way that felt immensely personal. To go beyond that, the side effect of that expression was to permanently and possibly fatally damage my new professional home and take the lives of hundreds of FDNY members and injure countless more. Moving out one level to the greater community, it felt the trauma too and suffered even more with thousands of deaths and injuries not just in New York but beyond. It was just too much for me to take in any way that allowed me to preserve any sense of my hope about my new home in particular and the world in general. It would take a long time for me to rebuild that hope and optimism to the extent that it could be rebuilt. Perhaps it is more accurate to say that events of that magnitude forever eliminate the old, and we are tasked to rebuild something that is actually entirely new from the rubble. Maybe the greatest miracle of our lives can be found when we are able to do this and to help our fellow humans do the same. But at the time, space was required and spending time at the epicenter of the shock or in events related to it was beyond what my heart, mind, and soul could endure.

Maybe that made me too sensitive; perhaps that meant I missed out on ways that I could have helped, but I found my way to serve in other places and in different roles. I poured myself into my work in the FDNY, taking as much overtime as I possibly could. I tried to find some path forward that allowed me to not fall too far into the emotional version of the pile and the pit that now occupied a large chunk of the lower part of the borough of Manhattan.

It was not conscious, but it was real. A big part of that path forward was very much connected to the tragedies that had occurred in my life before that point, even though those events were primarily personal. However, I had found myself navigating a way forward in those moments, too. Faced with the unimagined and the unimaginable, I had a choice, and the first element of that choice was to realize that I was not alone. Yet again, the connection to people and places would offer a way forward and highlight that one of the greatest gifts we are given in the face of tragedy is how other people help us endure our hardships. Whether a fire or a breakup, 9/11 or an assault, each event that tests us to the depths of our souls becomes an opportunity to connect and overcome.

21 | RETURNING TO NORMALCY?

Life proceeded in stops and starts in the weeks and months after 9/11. Everything that happened, including dates, paying bills, and navigating the roommate situation, slowly returned to an almost normal pace. However, there were things missing from the days that followed, for me and for many of the people I worked with. There was grief, sorrow, and mourning and many events designed to support that process. In the face of the number of them, there was no place to breathe, much less reflect or process. Nearly every day there was a firefighter, law enforcement or EMS funeral. There were community memorials in nearly every neighborhood. There was an interesting process of sharing the experiences of that day with friends who lived in New York and with friends and family from out of town. It all kind of balled together as the stories were shared and shared again. Helpful perhaps, but still too immediate and too immersive to be distinctive in most cases. What was most needed, but hardest to obtain, was perspective. That required distance and space from the events of the day.

I took two trips out of New York to gain some semblance of emotional room and work through what had happened. The first trip was to see my family, who had relocated temporarily to North Carolina. I spent two or three days hanging out with Mom, Dad, my sister, and the dog in their apartment on the northeast side of Charlotte. Unable or unwilling to process that my entire family had uprooted itself to pursue my sister's boyfriend and his family when they moved from Florida to North Carolina, I found a few opportunities to connect with my dad in ways I never had before. As a family, we were still processing my coming out experience, which had exploded on the day of my college graduation in 1999 and from which the genie had never come close to being put back in the bottle. Nevertheless, during those few short days, that entire topic was set aside in the face of the far more real challenges the world had just lived through. They affected me more directly than many, especially those not directly impacted.

My dad had always talked about his service as a medic in Vietnam in the way families talk about a trip taken before children entered the picture. Dad had photo albums and a few gentle stories about his military service, including when an overzealous military policeman gave him a ticket for going just a little over the speed limit. This cost him his good conduct medal and perhaps created the mindset that led to my father never speeding to this day, over fifty years later.

In the afterworld of the attacks, however, my dad and I discussed Vietnam in real terms for the first time. He related some of the experiences that would not have been covered in family postcards back home. He shared some of the fear and the frustration that he experienced, especially as Medic assigned first to helicopters and then later to river boats. In that role, he had been faced with the worst of the worst and had to find something inside to allow him to continue despite fear and danger. Although his danger was obviously far more physical and immediate than mine, being a part of an experience that generated all kinds of scars was something he understood well. It was fascinating to me that in the face of so much destruction, a new bridge had been created between generations—between father and son, and between his trauma and mine. We were mutually supportive and accepting in ways that we had never been before, owing to the differences between us and our personalities, differences that had been exacerbated by my coming out. From that moment forward, our bond would be different, even if we never acknowledged it specifically. For the rest of my family, it was status quo, although that trip would be the first stop on a path that would lead to acceptance and support. In a few years, it would lead to open invitations for my partner to visit my family and even stay in their home. These things take time, and sometimes they take moments of clarity, like the tiny silver linings in the shadows of the darkest clouds that just won't go away.

My other refuge in the aftermath was found on a visit home to the friends I had left behind in Columbus. One evening, they held a birthday party for me, and we ended up at one of those "fast casual" restaurants that can be a good experience occasionally. The conversations were welcome, and the stories were intense, but it was a necessary part of healing. Spending time with firefighter friends who understood the basics of the world I worked in offered a chance to verbalize some of what had happened on the 11ᵗʰ and in the days that followed. It was somewhat therapeutic but as operations were still ongoing, it was only temporary relief. Most of all, it was just good to be around friends and away from the middle of the environment for a few days. On the way to the airport to head back to New York, while sitting in a Waffle House celebrating another friend's birthday (who happened to be a Columbus firefighter), the restaurant began to buzz while raised and worried voices asked about "it" happening again. That was the morning American Airlines Flight 587 crashed in the Rockaway section of Queens, one of the deadliest non-terrorist related aviation accidents in American history. It happened only two months and a day after 9/11. In a moment of supreme coincidence, the supervising dispatcher for the Queens plane crash was the same person who had been the supervisor in Manhattan on the morning of September 11. He had been granted a transfer to Queens after September 11 as a form of "break" from the activity level, a break that did not prove much of a break at all, at least on November 12. It seemed like a dream, especially since I was on my way to an airport to fly back to New York. It was a relief,

I suppose, when the news announced that this was likely not a terrorist attack. It's a strange source of relief to know that horrible tragedies can happen for all kinds of reasons and, sometimes, for seemingly no reason at all. I made my way back to New York, comforted by time with friends, and fell back into a routine of work that continued to move slowly toward our new normal.

22 | MARCH 11, 2002

By March of 2002, the city had started to return to its almost everyday normal. Strangers were not quite so kind; many of the impromptu memorials, like the photos at Union Square, had been taken down, and the fires had long since burned out. The city had a new mayor, Michael Bloomberg. Efforts were already picking up steam to rebuild Lower Manhattan and ensure that whatever would be there was a fitting tribute not just to those who had been lost, but also to the damaged senses of pride and security of New York and the United States of America. I had gone back for the last part of the dispatcher training school, completed decision dispatcher training and been assigned my permanent dispatcher number. I went from Dispatcher 801 to Dispatcher 466 and held that number until I was promoted to Supervising Dispatcher in January 2003.

The funerals continued as members were identified, and I developed a habit of volunteering to cover the work of anyone who wanted to go to a funeral. I hated funerals ever since I was a kid. I had refused to go to my beloved grandmother's funeral in 1984, staying at my aunt's house instead and munching on Shake Shoppe French fries in the care of a babysitter. My disdain for facing death would remain a fundamental personality trait for the duration of my time in New York, even though I would end up attending many funerals for co-workers and family members in the years after 2001. Life has a way of forcing you to face what you sincerely wish not to face. In early 2002, the routine was still full of 9/11 related events and activities. The routes of the subways were still changed, the operations of the FDNY were still impacted, and we were still in the midst of the trauma response, unable to grieve in any real way. In essence, the emergency continued for all those in the Fire Department, regardless of their capacity or role, while the surrounding population largely got their routines back in place.

However, in a very unexpected way, our emotional stasis was finally altered by a documentary aired in commemoration of the six-month anniversary of September 11. Hosted by Robert DeNiro, the documentary featured the work of a team of French filmmakers who had been riding along with Lower Manhattan fire companies on the morning of September 11. They were on the scene of a gas leak near the Twin Towers when the first plane struck. They filmed much of the incident's initial hours: the rescue efforts, the victims, including those who threw themselves from the upper floors, and the subsequent collapse and aftermath. It served as the fundamental diary of that day's events. Even so many years later, I can still remember the feelings of pride and release, but also sadness generated by the film. It was like looking at an old home movie reel before something changed everything—before Mom and Dad divorced, brother Tim died, or the house burned down, and the dog ran away. It was a window back to something that was forever lost that day for all of us. It's a strange place to be. It reminded me of the feeling of that time and place. Of the wonder that existed in what was largely a period of hope about what potential existed for me in New York and which was robbed in the aftermath of the Tower's fall. It was a loss of innocence moment, immortalized for all of us on camera and shown for millions who each had their own relationship to that Tuesday morning.

What made their footage and program even more powerful was what they recorded before 9/11. While watching, I remembered I had met them a month or two before at the Manhattan central office one day when I was working there on a detail (when a dispatcher is sent from an office with extra people for a shift to an office that is short of people). The company that had visited the Manhattan office that day was Rescue Company One and included their captain, Terry Hatton. The documentary featured many of the members who were lost. It was filmed on the scene of emergencies and fires and in conversations around the firehouse or during training. It also captured something else, more subtle but perhaps even more real. Much like the footage of Pearl Harbor from right before the attack on December 7 or the footage of the *Challenger* astronauts walking to the shuttle before that terrible explosion in 1986, you could see what was right before a shock so great it shifted the world. The world was one way in one moment and a few minutes later, after the sounds of explosions, screams, and shattering falling glass, it was so much different. It was like watching the Big Bang and seeing the genesis of the world come to focus in an instant.

That documentary, aired to help millions better understand the events of 9/11, also helped to illustrate the worlds of 9/10 and 9/12. Right there, in scenes of firehouse conversations, the voices of dispatchers, and the responses to routine emergencies and fires right up to 8:47 a.m. on September 11, 2001, you could see what life in the FDNY was like. In the debris, the cries, the smoke, and the fire of the minutes and hours after the first plane hit, you could see a world completely changed. None of my friends at work had processed what had happened until watching that documentary, which, thankfully, my group had the opportunity to do in the safety and security of our homes. I think we were all still so wrapped up in the mode of action and doing the job that we had either neglected, or avoided, the inevitable emotional reckoning. We came in the next day for a night shift, and before long, it was the topic of all conversation. More than a few people admitted that in the shadow of those scenes, we found the space to grieve and admit in rather hushed tones to each other that we finally had faced the reality of that day and its aftermath.

The conversation about the documentary did not last long. As I recall, it did not even extend across the entire shift. However, for a little while, framed by the scenes and voices contained within that special program, we found common ground upon which to reflect and grieve at least a little about what had happened. It is not reasonable or realistic to describe or even guess what passed as the grieving process for a community of 200 dispatchers, 13,000 members of the FDNY, or the millions of people who lived in the New York region. But it is fair to suspect that the path forward was largely made of the scenes and situations, tasks and toils of the jobs that still needed to be done. The same jobs as before 9/11 which could be a path to move beyond the trauma of 9/11.

People will always need help, and no matter how terrible the events of 9/11 were, reminding ourselves of that fact was the closest thing we had to a map for the way forward or out. When in doubt, go to what you know or find familiar. That was exactly what the daily challenges of fires and emergencies, phone calls and training, overtime, and coffee offered us. Was it the healthiest approach? Probably not, but it was something to ground us and guide us, and that was what we needed most of all: a map back to someplace safe, or at least safer than where we had been.

23 | JUNE 2002

That was the way things progressed for the next year. Bit by bit, life returned to its previous ways of being, although we knew that things would never really be "normal" again. For me, one of the things that had been altered by the aftermath of 9/11 was the person I had started to date a few months after the attack. We had met in a manner that today seems antiquated: an AOL chat room. He had interests like mine, and our online conversations were easy and engaging. We agreed to meet in person at a subway station in downtown Brooklyn. Subsequently, we had one of those magical first date evenings of wandering the streets, chatting effortlessly, and me convincing myself that this was the "one." Our relationship would not last long, ending dramatically on the dance floor of a club in Brooklyn called Spectrum. It was infamous as the spot where the characters danced on a lighted disco dance floor in *Saturday Night Fever*.

Pride weekend of 2002, I had moved by myself (thankfully) into a new apartment in Bay Ridge. We were supposed to meet at Spectrum that night to celebrate the place. When he failed to show up at the agreed time and did not bother to text, call, or otherwise provide any clue of what was happening, I knew something was up. Finally, a couple of hours later, he arrived, walked up to me, handed me the apartment key I had given him, turned around, and walked out. Not a word was said.

In the years after that moment, as I tried to maintain some sort of friendship with this person who had gone from future husband to personal dating horror story in just a few short months, it became clear that, in many ways, our relationship was a 9/11 aftershock. He was self-diagnosed with Asperger's; I do not know if it was ever officially verified. No matter what his officially diagnosed condition was, he often lacked empathy or compassion for others. Affection was a forced struggle, to say nothing of more physical entanglements. I suspect that our relationship was something he needed to move on from 9/11 and the feelings it created in him. When he spoke of watching the towers burn from a distant spot that morning, it was the only time I saw him ever come close to crying. He had suffered a hard and difficult life as a child, and it would likely not be wrong to suspect the lack of a warm upbringing helped to create a cold adult. Everyone reacts to tragedy in his or her own way—but the individual does react. It is amazing to me, looking back, that the cure for the bigger pain for him and so many others was to try and find love in the micro. As the greater hurt prevailed, he (and we) fell back into our bad habits and shut the door on one of the best things to provide relief in the face of the scale of tragedies both small and immense.

The further we progressed in time from 9/11, the more he retreated from me and back into his old self. Ultimately, he denied that anything had existed between us, despite his very real effort to stay friends for decades after. He could never explain why, but it would be the arrival of another terrible time, the pandemic of 2020, when he would text me one day and state finally that he recognized what it could have been and that he wished it could have worked out.

By then, I was twenty years moved on and years into a wonderful relationship with someone else who would become my husband. I shared this text from the past with him, and he asked what I thought about it. I shared that I was deeply and profoundly sad that the best parts of my long-gone ex could only, apparently, be revealed in the face of tragedies or challenges so extreme and so much time and distance. I was also saddened by the fact that I know others who suffer from the same affliction. We are so disconnected from others in the day to day that it too often takes an extreme event to remind us we are all connected, whether as friends, lovers, or members of a community. In this way, my ex reflected all of New York City, a city of determined isolation until something really shitty happens, and then it's all aboard the lifeboats. These boats are often in the shape of other people who otherwise we might not even give the time of day, only to abandon the lifeboats at the first sign of the safety of shore.

Back in 2002, the very next morning after the night of the silent, dramatic, lighted dance floor breakup was the New York City Pride Parade. This experience was, and remains, in many ways the pinnacle of the gay life in the United States. Hours of floats and marchers, hundreds of thousands of onlookers, and a glorious reminder of the vitality of living into one's truth about who God made them to be. In June of 2002, it included one marcher who had been two years in New York City from a slightly less grandiose city in the Midwest.

At some point in my early time in New York City, I joined a group called Fire-Flag. It was a professional group for LGBTQ firefighters, emergency medical professionals, and dispatchers. I attended several meetings, made a few friends, and marched with the group in the 2002 Pride Parade. We were co-grand marshals along with the Gay Officer's Action League (GOAL). They were the equivalent of our organization, primarily made up of members of the New York City Police Department and other regional law enforcement organizations. The entire experience was a bit of a blur. Mayor Michael Bloomberg walked alongside us down the parade route through the streets of Manhattan to the parade's conclusion at the Pride Festival in Greenwich Village. This was just a block away from where my guardian angel of a friend had given me her guided tour of gay New York just three years before.

As each cluster of amassed parade watchers figured out who we were, the cheers erupted from street level and cascaded down from those on balconies and rooftops. It was a collective thank you from our community that paled compared to anything I would ever experience as workplace recognition. It was heartwarming to the point of overwhelming to be recognized at the same time for so many different things—not just for our sexual orientation and being "out" at work, of course, but for our service to the community. For those of us who work in the public safety world, the service nature of our identities and calling is often, and maybe always, primary to any other, including our sexual orientations. It was clear that there was so much appreciation and gratitude in those amazingly boisterous crowds, still partly in shadow from the events of nine months before.

I had debated going. I had vacillated on even trying to attend one Fire-Flag meeting. I had made my career to this point out of not leading with my differences. I tried carefully to navigate being myself, but I also did not make myself stand out to the point that my chosen home would be taken from me because I was too different to remain.

It was never and would never be all "easy" to be an out gay person working in the fire department. Even if others were fine with me, there was always an undercurrent of worry and self-doubt. I do know that as much as I was able, I controlled the controllables and tried to ensure that I led first with who I was as a whole person: dedicated to my profession, committed to my co-workers, and passionate about service. Maybe I went overboard sometimes, and perfectionism was and remains a sin with which I am intimately familiar. Still, I was, to my mind, mostly successful in balancing who I was. Fortunately, my immediate co-workers, motivated initially by my first supervisor, never gave me much grief at all. I will forever be convinced that the gay issue was largely inconsequential, at least as far as I knew. Odd then that on a brilliant June Sunday, in a city that was still reverberating from the unimaginable shocks of nine months before, I felt celebrated and acknowledged, not for one part of me, but rather for the entire person by one million strangers who would likely never know my name much less all the events that had brought me to that place and time.

In the face of the long delay between when I "knew" and when I started the process of coming out, I wondered what I would have done differently if I had known how it would turn out. I wondered if the understanding that there would be a supportive place in the world for me would have brought about the admission earlier. I also could not help thinking about the crazy way that a tragedy of global proportions was now inexorably linked to my growth as a person—and a heartbreak not even twenty-four hours old. It was my life in a nutshell and New York City in a microcosm. It was all of the ups, downs, and sideways events compressed in time and place and still colored by the events of a September only nine months in the past.

24 | SEPTEMBER 11, 2002

The year 2002 brought significant changes to my work environment, not just in our recovery from 9/11 but also in my personal experience. I had developed a bit of a troublemaker reputation in the Brooklyn central office. Perhaps this was because I had many opinions about things or did not always go smoothly with the flow. I had been moved from my assignment in the Brooklyn office to a different group (sort of a warning shot of sorts) and then, later on, moved out of Brooklyn entirely and assigned to the Bronx. This was the type of action that had been taken previously because department leadership wanted to either change our attitudes or drive us out of the job entirely. I had never been written up or given a bad evaluation. No one ever sat me down and said that I was doing anything wrong, but I was not afraid to speak up. As a new person, that was one of the gravest sins anyone could commit. The behavior correction process was subtle, and it was only in hushed tones that my concerned co-workers and friends revealed to me my potential deficiencies.

Despite this, there I was, reporting to work in the Bronx central office—a two-hour subway ride from home—which meant leaving the apartment in Bay Ridge around 4:30 a.m. on day tours. It was tough, but I enjoyed learning about a new part of New York City. I proved my capabilities and skills early on, winning praise from an especially salty supervisor when I directed responding units to an updated drowning location without being told to do so by anyone else. It was just common sense for me, but this classic tough guy, the FDNY supervising dispatcher, found it a special enough moment to walk over and inform me directly and personally that I had done well. For me, that was as good as a medal, and I knew then that I would be okay no matter where I ended up. Maybe today the transfer and the mystery around why would warrant official complaints and inquiries, but I accepted it as part of the job. I was still new, still needed to prove myself, and still planned on leaving anyway for a master's degree and brighter pastures beyond the fire department.

This began to change as I learned about the job in the Bronx, developed a love of the traditions of the FDNY, and began to understand the true story of how our group played such an important role in the safety of the city. That occurred in the months after 9/11, and I started considering the potential for staying in the job longer than planned. That adjustment to my plan would be solidified by the events marking the first anniversary of 9/11.

The traditional reading of the "four fives" had been held off for months. There were just too many names, and it would have been a detriment to the daily operations and focus of the department to engage in almost daily readings. The decision was made to announce all 343 names on September 11, 2002. I was working in the Bronx that day. We were to read the names of those lost in one massive announcement over the FDNY voice-alarm (intercom) system starting at 08:47 hours. As our shift discussed who should do it and how, we agreed that three of us would share the duties as a tribute—recognizing that it was so much more than a one-person job every day, much less on September 11, 2001. The morning was beautiful, much like it had been the year before.

I had not made plans to celebrate my birthday that day; it would be many years before I dared to have birthday events on the actual day. Even decades later, I find it difficult to celebrate on the day, preferring to do any birthday festivities before or after. That morning, the focus was on reading these names—and doing it well. Pronunciations were practiced along with timing. We made sure the background noise would be at a minimum. The designated time arrived, and the process began. At the moment the announcement began, the wind outside began to howl. They had been completely calm right up until the tone alert sounded. The howl would continue, at least where we were in the Bronx, until the last name was read over an hour later. With the message's conclusion, the winds died down and everyone in the office sighed. A person or two may have shed a tear. Everyone, without question, thought about where we had been and what had happened not just one year ago that day, but in the days and hours since. We reflected with sadness and pride that we had done the job well and worked hard to help our department and city recover.

In time, I would see that same truth in everyone I knew, and many I did not know. It was most clearly visible in the faces, voices, anger, and sadness of my co-workers at FDNY who would manage the response to the greatest terror attack America has ever known—hopefully, the greatest we will ever know. It was visible in the faces of those who had to manage the aftermath. It was also visible in those who lived and worked in New York, the unfortunate millions who experienced the attack firsthand and the days after when we collectively navigated our way forward as a community. At the one-year mark, there was still so much to be done, but there was also the understanding that we had come so far, and we had only been able to do that because of what we could do together.

In terms of FDNY dispatch, this group of people, who I would eventually come to lead as their director, brought their own experiences to bear on a beautiful Tuesday morning in the year 2001 to bring some sense of order out of unspeakable chaos. On a day when so many others found themselves compelled to shut down, two hundred women and men, black and white, gay and straight, senior and junior, kind and not so kind—all of them, in all their multitudes, showed up and did the job. They talked to people trapped in towers who knew that it was the end, even if they could not say it. They helped firefighters trapped in buildings, coordinated the first ever large-scale mutual aid response into the city of New York, and ensured things got done. They did all this with training but no planning. There was no big red binder on a dusty shelf to guide us in what to do. There were also no high-ranking chiefs to call on for guidance. It was all invented, created on the fly—and it was a miracle.

So many were lost that day—firefighters and civilians—but so many more were saved. I remember well the first newspaper headlines that estimated 10,000 dead. The number would be more than 70 percent less. It is hard to think of losing over 2000 people as a success, but in some ways, it most certainly was. It is even harder to think of losing 343 firefighters as anything like a success. Still, that sacrifice saved so many thousands of people. It will hopefully forever be the greatest rescue operation in history—an operation only ended by the greatest collapses of buildings as the result of fire in human history.

The story of how those women and men in FDNY's fire dispatch central offices accomplished their superhuman efforts is not overly complex. Still, it is critically important for any high-performance organization to understand. It offers significant insight into how organizations and people can accomplish great things today and in the future. However, that story is also tied to the truth of anyone who has dreamed, faced adversity, and learned that only with a group of supporters, friends, colleagues, family, and community can we accomplish something that others might label impossible. That is a lesson we would learn again in my time in New York, one instance notably a direct consequence of September 11, six years later.

25 | DEUTSCHE BANK, AUGUST 2007

The voice on the other end of the line was one of desperation, almost as much desperation as you would sometimes hear from callers reporting severe fires. They were asking one of the most critical questions that a supervisor in the FDNY ever could, especially on a beautiful summer weekend: "Would you please come in and cover an overtime spot in the Manhattan communications office?" It was a summer afternoon in August. My sister and her boyfriend (soon-to-be husband) were visiting, and I did not want to work. By this time in 2007, I was assigned to the training unit. I worked a Monday to Friday schedule and enjoyed having a more regular cadence to my week. I also did not want to give up the chance to earn overtime, so I devised a plan. My sister and her boyfriend would ride with me to the Manhattan central office. I would work the 1:00 p.m. to 7:00 p.m. overtime shift while they explored Central Park, went to a museum or two, and found ways to occupy themselves. At 7:00 p.m., they would meet me back at the CO, and we would go to a nice dinner in the city. I convinced myself this plan would work wonderfully. I should have known better.

The first two and a half hours were tranquil. By the time 3:30 p.m. rolled around, there was not a single active fire department response in the borough of Manhattan. It was hard to stay awake in the quiet and dark office, and I had become bored. There were people to talk to, of course. Our staffing was seven dispatchers and a supervisor, but that day's tour was a cast of people who never regularly worked together. There were a couple of folks just out of training. There were some others on overtime, like me, and there was at least one detail—a dispatcher sent from another office with extra staffing. This hodge podge crew had never worked together—ever. I considered that if we did get busy, it would be interesting to see how it would go.

My curiosity was answered at 3:36 p.m. when a single 911 line lit up, indicating an incoming phone call. Even though I was a supervisor and answering the emergency phone was not something I was supposed to do, boredom had set in, and I was right by a phone. So I answered it using the same scripted beginning as I had been trained almost seven years before: "Fire Department, Dispatcher 45, what is the address of the fire?" The voice on the other end was clearly terrified. Her words were haunting and past the place of screaming or yelling to express the need for help. "I am standing at the corner of Greenwich and Cedar. And that building that was hit on 9/11, the whole top ten floors of it are…on fire."

It was an August afternoon; it was sunny outside. There were thousands of people in this area, and this was the only call reporting this in the middle of New York. *Wait*, I asked myself. *Could only one person see this?* I did not let my doubts slow my handling of the call or what I entered into the computer, but that doubt was present, nonetheless. In less than forty seconds, her report had been processed with enough information to dispatch the fire department. As much as the lack of other calls made me think this was likely a bogus call, I could not help but be affected by the tone of her voice, her halting words, and the way she drew out every syllable to ensure I understood her completely. I ended the phone call with our scripted statement—"The fire department will respond"—and released the incident to my fellow dispatcher for processing.

As the decision dispatcher read the comments and ensured the correct response, I looked up the Critical Incident Dispatch System information to verify what I had suspected. This fire was, in fact, reported to be at the Deutsche Bank Building. Located directly across the street from where the Twin Towers had stood, this building took significant damage from the flying debris on September 11, 2001. On this day, it was in the midst of undergoing a multi-year demolition process, partly due to the damage and partly due to asbestos and other hazardous materials in the structure. Now, years after 9/11, this building, too, was reportedly on fire.

Within just a few seconds, we knew that the caller had been extremely accurate with her report. Waves of phone calls began arriving at the central office, so many that other boroughs also had to answer calls reporting this major fire in Lower Manhattan. Less than a minute after dispatching the fire companies, the first arriving unit, responding from the firehouse across the street, shared its initial report: "10-75, we have fire in a highrise building." This was followed shortly thereafter by a report they had flaming debris falling down all sides of the structure and for all responding units to use extreme caution.

Within one minute, all hell had broken loose in the office and on the narrow streets of Lower Manhattan. Within moments, the fire escalated to a fourth alarm high-rise fire, one of FDNY's most significant responses. Simultaneously with ensuring the appropriate response to the fire, answering phone calls reporting the event from all over Lower Manhattan, and the relocation of fire companies to cover now empty firehouses, the dispatchers of FDNY processed other alarms and gave a clinic on what it means to be an effective team. They did this as literal strangers to each other, a team of professionals who did not have the gift of regular collaboration to support making quick decisions or picking up on non-verbal clues. This random collection of dispatch personnel managed the movement of over one hundred pieces of fire apparatus from all five city boroughs, while communicating, coordinating, documenting, and bringing a sense of ordered professionalism to the chaos. It was as though an entire football team of free agents suddenly appeared to play in the Super Bowl. Each man and woman on the shift that day did remarkable work to ensure that this increasingly complex fire of massive proportions was handled along with all of the other tasks.

However, the fire took a dark turn about an hour into the event. A radio report from the scene stated that many firefighters had become trapped on the upper floors of the building in the process of trying to extinguish the fire. Hi-rise fires are challenging enough, but the nature of this building (it was under demolition, the stairways and elevators were removed, and the standpipes were inoperative) meant that the firefight was an almost impossible challenge. Still, the firefighters had made their best efforts to extinguish the fire. Then, their efforts had to change to focus on rescuing their now-trapped brethren. The report of a "mayday," or firefighter in trouble, is one of the most alarming phrases any fire dispatcher can hear over a radio. However, realizing how bad this fire was only motivated the on-duty dispatchers to elevate their performance further.

The mayday signal necessitated even more resources, including many units from outside Manhattan. This amount of coordination and communication demanded a level of skill, knowledge, and proficiency that exemplified what FDNY dispatchers can do on their best days. Although the rescue efforts at the scene were extensive and heroic beyond measure, sadly, two FDNY firefighters did not survive—becoming, in many ways, delayed casualties of 9/11.

It was important then, as it is now, to acknowledge the tragic loss of the two firefighters that day. Still, it is also essential to recognize the heroic performance of the dispatchers who processed the calls, managed the response, and did not do their work that day in vain, despite the tragic loss of members. Although there were miracles on Liberty Street that day, the miracle was incomplete. It is a hard truth of a life and career in public safety that, sometimes, not everyone gets to go home. Sometimes, our best is not good enough. It is an incomplete and largely ineffective source of comfort or pride to try to find some solace in knowing that "it could have been worse," but that was true in the case of not just the Deutsche Bank fire but in so many other events that I experienced in FDNY.

The efforts of those in the FDNY central offices and in the field made things better, and helped more people survive than likely would have. Those efforts were not and could not have been perfect. For anyone working in a field where perfection is too often expected, this is the start of the slippery slope that can lead to all types of horrible side effects and outright mental health crises. The first antidote is cultural. Develop an understanding that just because something terrible happened does not discount everything else that happened which was good. There is a balance between a desire to be perfect and an acknowledgment that we cannot be. We don't want to stop trying for the loftiest of goals, but we don't want to destroy ourselves in the face of goals that were not realistic in the first place. Goals which are, in the end, unattainable.

In the days and weeks after this fire, in the aftermath of the funerals of the two firefighters, the department itself needed to recognize this truth. Thankfully, the department officially commended those dispatchers for their efforts to support those on the scene and ensure resources for other events. This went a long way to helping the dispatchers navigate that treacherous place between understanding the outcome was by no means ideal and recognizing their efforts were far above their ordinary course of duty.

In reflection, this understanding was one of the most critical insights of my career in FDNY. There is a need to acknowledge whenever team members go above and beyond, especially when operating only from a foundation of shared experience and training, not regular familiarity. It is also important to acknowledge that sometimes miracles can be fickle and that trying to understand why or how is best left to higher powers than those we possess. This is also a universal truth for all those who work in public safety, whether under a headset, on a fire engine, in a patrol car, or in an ambulance. To have any hope of avoiding becoming a casualty to our passionate commitment to do the most heroic job possible, we must find a healthy way forward when things do not work out. That is true whether you work in the City of New York or at the smallest rural agency. Tragedy and its impacts can be universal and demand attention, diligence, support, and care to overcome.

26 | SUPERSTORM SANDY

One of my life's most intense work experiences, in many ways more challenging than the blackout or even 9/11 in terms of operations, began for me in Roanoke, Virgina in late October 2012. I was there, attending a training conference, when it became apparent that a powerful tropical storm system would come very close to New York City. This was not a new occurrence for our organization. A year before, Tropical Storm Hanna had made landfall as a weakening tropical storm on Coney Island in Brooklyn. The forecast had been for the storm to be more serious, which meant we had made intense preparations in coordination with FDNY operational staff. Plans were developed, additional units deployed, and when the big moment happened, it largely failed to meet expectations. The tropical storm had lessened in intensity a bit, which meant only the borough of Queens saw a spike in activity. The heaviest of the rain bands shifted to the west and ended up causing disastrous flooding in New England, leaving the city of New York largely spared.

Some agencies and organizations have a mindset that a prepared-for but unrealized disaster is one of the best possible opportunities for training and preparation. It has all the prep work but none of the pain. That was my mindset about it as well. From tropical storm Hanna, just like from the blackout of 2003, I personally documented lessons learned and insights gained from what happens when a disaster threatens a major American metropolis. This event offered specific examples related to tropical storms—lessons that may be familiar to agencies farther south in places like Florida or the Carolinas, but which were mainly foreign to New Yorkers and their fire department.

Unfortunately, the failure to meet potential was not viewed the same way by everyone I worked with, especially some of the leaders in my part of the fire department. They viewed our efforts at planning for Hanna as a waste of time and resources and validation of their belief that major tropical storm systems would only affect the city of New York with a little rain and wind. Now, a year later, as this new storm's path came into more certainty, I decided to cut short my trip to Virginia to go home to New York. Reports by the scientists and hurricane experts indicated that something dire may be about to happen in the New York City region. While traveling home, I engaged in a flurry of excited phone conversations with my fellow FDNY chief dispatchers about what type of planning was being done to get us ready. I knew that if we waited too long, it would be too late to get extra people, take care of personnel who had family concerns, and ensure effective operations.

Several things became apparent when I made it back to the city and reported for an overtime shift as the citywide chief dispatcher on a Sunday day tour. First, yet again, we would need the skills and talent of the dispatchers working in the central offices to develop plans on the fly and adapt to what was to come. The type of comprehensive dispatch plan implemented for tropical storm Hanna in 2011 had not been replicated for this storm. It would be largely improvised, and that would have to be enough.

On Monday afternoon, as Superstorm Sandy approached, we received our first clue as to the events to come. A construction crane, eighty stories above the streets of Midtown Manhattan, snapped and dangled precariously over nearby buildings. From that moment forward, the women and men of FDNY fire dispatch operations, alongside their colleagues from NYPD911 and radio, as well as FDNY Emergency Medical Dispatch, would process thousands of calls for service from across the five boroughs.

Entire neighborhoods would be cut off by floodwaters. Sadly, people would drown in their homes, a few of them while on the phone with FDNY dispatchers attempting to help them while trying to guide field responders to their locations. This was often an impossible task and again, like on September 11, 2001, dispatchers worked through unimaginable conversations with callers and response scenarios while worried about their own loved ones. What made this event even worse was the number of FDNY dispatchers whose own homes and families were in peril from the floodwaters.

Approximately twenty of the two hundred personnel who worked for FDNY fire dispatch suffered severe damage to their homes. Several had to coordinate the rescue of their own family members while on duty. Other events continued, from notifications of hospitals flooding to building collapses and many fires. One fire burned an entire section of the Rockaway Peninsula in Queens. While the teams of dispatchers, supervisors, and chief dispatchers worked to manage the insane volume of calls and support the units in the field, there were more than a few debates about how much we could adjust response policies to match our available resources.

At one point, a now-retired member of our dispatch leadership staff demanded that we continue to respond to calls for wires down. Not only would this have quickly exhausted all our available resources, but the winds had increased to a point where it was not safe to have responders in the field, much less attempt to mitigate electrical conditions in the middle of rising water. Luckily, his boss understood the consequences of such an action, and dispatchers were empowered to make the best possible decisions about where to send our increasingly limited resources. People often assume that FDNY, with over 189 engine companies and over 140 ladder companies along with an armada of chiefs, special operations units, and other units at its disposal, can handle just about any event. That is true 99 percent of the time. However, on the three primary days impacted by Superstorm Sandy, it was not uncommon to have almost no units available in the entire city. That had not even happened on September 11, 2001, when approximately 50 percent of the FDNY's resources were available for other emergencies. During Sandy, however, the size, scale, and scope were unbelievably different.

The event would also prove a turning point in another way. A series of conversations between myself and the same manager who wanted us to respond to every wires-down call would serve to launch my professional emergency communications career in a new direction. As events wound down, the extent of damage done to the city became clear, as well as the potential impact on the fire dispatch personnel who had managed the event. I reached out to my manager to ask that the fire department counseling unit be requested to come to our dispatch center to speak with the dispatch team. Today, this sort of counseling process is an accepted industry practice in most agencies. The goal is to have trained counselors speak with dispatch personnel about the event and help ensure they do not suffer from post-traumatic stress disorder. Counselors provide information about what resources are available should dispatchers need additional assistance and make return visits in the weeks after a serious event to follow-up. In this case, the dispatchers of the FDNY had just dispatched over 33,000 incidents in thirty-six hours (about fifteen times the normal rate) and answered countless phone calls from stranded, trapped, and, in some cases, dying people.

My manager's answer to my request was incredulous: "What do you think you are, some kind of psychologist?" I tried to explain to him the lessons I had learned from the conferences I had started attending on my own. (The Bureau of Communications was not engaged in outside professional education or training at that time.) It was clear that events of this magnitude demanded this type of support for our personnel. I became increasingly angry at the indifference and lack of compassion he showed for the people he was supposed to lead. When he said, "I think the only person who needs help is you," I slammed down the phone, shaking in rage and frustration.

After a few seconds, I remembered that a member of the fire dispatcher's union was working on the floor that shift. I decided to share with them my request, thinking they would immediately see its value. I asked them to make the call on behalf of the union, of which I was a member. The response shredded any calm I had reclaimed: "We did not need any help after 9/11. I don't see why they need any help now." I was dumbfounded. To have not one but two people express such a profoundly shortsighted view of the need to take care of employees in the face of disaster and trauma was more than I could bear. I stomped back to my office, slammed the door, and turned off the lights. In what was probably the defining moment of my career, I made the call myself, insubordination charges or frustrated union leaders be damned.

Thankfully, the counseling unit showed up quickly and repeatedly over the next weeks. They did exactly what they were supposed to do, checking in on people from their position of trusted and trained outsider. That old-school mentality of people not needing help or that receiving help is a sign of weakness is largely gone today from even traditional organizations. Despite the retrospective view that these two individuals' actions were horrific in many ways, it is important to acknowledge that they were operating from a position in a world that they knew. They had never received training in mental health concerns for dispatchers. At that time, to my knowledge, they had never attended a 911 industry conference or learned about the trends in the industry around mental health or PTSD. I took that awareness for granted. In the face of the stress of that day, I failed to appreciate that in the face of such a universally stressful event, we were going to retreat back to what we knew best. The comfort of a traditional mindset and historical experience was powerful for my boss and the union leader. It made it easier for them to make it through that time. Had I been able to better share or explain, it might have helped them make a better decision.

It is almost funny, in retrospect, to compare a team's performance when everyone has a common operational perspective or framework compared to when one team member has new or different information. If the person with the up-to-date insights is unable or unwilling to share that information in a way that permits the other members to integrate that information into their process, or if that new information is so different that it threatens the other team members' framework of security, then it becomes a no-win scenario. Both sides are doomed to see things from their points of view and will be highly resistant to changing their opinions or tactics. This challenge plagues all organizations, especially those operating in high-stakes, high-stress environments. Communication and trust are the keys. If there is an effort to get people to a new place of understanding, much like any journey involving travel, you have to understand where you and the other parties started and where you need them to go. If you can effectively understand those components of the process and the obstacles and opportunities found on that journey, you can start to communicate in a way that helps people see the new thing less as a threat and more as an opportunity. You can get people to accept they need to do something new or different because it will benefit them and, potentially, those they care about.

That level of understanding was beyond my capacity in 2012, and I will not suggest I am anywhere near perfect at it now. As a result, all these years later, I can say that my boss was right: I did need help but not of a psychiatric kind, instead of a leadership kind which is certainly not how he intended his cutting remark.

Thankfully, as an industry, the public safety community, including dispatch and 911, has evolved in its position since 2012. A review of LinkedIn and social media clearly illustrates that many public safety communications organizations around the United States and beyond take the emotional well-being of their personnel very seriously, not just in the face of the worst days, but as a continuous effort to support their most valuable resources. In the face of the storm, that was my key takeaway. Along the way, I also gleaned a clue about where the world was headed. In the middle of the event, when the call volume was at its highest, we received a phone call from FDNY headquarters that someone had "tweeted" that they needed help. An intern working on the still-new social media effort saw this message and she had no idea what to do with the report. What happened to the person who tweeted their request for help has faded from memory. Still, the dawn of a new era has led us to a day where phone calls to report emergencies are becoming increasingly quaint, archaic, and inefficient. With the combination of artificial intelligence, sensors, smart watches, door cameras, and many other technologies, it is possible that someday many or even most emergencies will be reported without human interaction, likely within a few years.

Superstorm Sandy offered a vision of the human and technological trends of the future in the face of a disaster unprecedented in its scale, scope, and legacy. However, in all the ways that Superstorm Sandy was different, it was another validation of something as traditional as horses and fire poles. The storm, its aftermath, and the work by the dispatchers of FDNY highlighted yet again what was possible with a well-trained, skilled, and knowledgeable team of public safety professionals. Events like Deutsche Bank, the Blackout, and Superstorm Sandy were not unique except, perhaps, in geography or scale. They were simply the best examples of what those women and men could do every single day should such challenges arise. That does not mean they were perfect; no organization made up of human beings ever is. However, the willingness to rise to a challenge, make critical decisions, apply creativity and insight to manage complex events, and take pride and ownership in their work was there every day. When there was only one fire during a shift or when there were twenty—or a superstorm—they handled it all.

27 | FOR WHAT PURPOSE?

All the hard, difficult professional and personal experiences of my life came to their ultimate expression in the events surrounding September 11, 2001. That day, for so many reasons, stands out as the most extreme example possible of what it meant to be on a team of the world's greatest fire dispatchers serving the world's greatest fire department. Although the best of what the organization did on that day was reflected in many other events and continues to be reflected today in incidents both significant and routine, that beautiful, horrible September morning reflects so much more than one moment in our collective history. September 11th, 2001 serves as the best and most terrible example of the power of community and connection to help us overcome the most trying of our days—whether the tragedies are felt only by one or by millions.

September 11th, 2001 put the professionalism and capabilities of the women and men of FDNY Fire Dispatch on a stage for the world to see. It is not the nature of public safety communications professionals to boast about what they do. More often than not, their impact is nearly forgotten or is, at best, an afterthought. However, after 9/11, as the audio tapes and the stories about the response and actions after the collapse aired on TV, people responded with attention and appreciation for what the dispatchers of the FDNY had done. A slow process began that ultimately led to Dispatchers being acknowledged at FDNY award ceremonies, featured in social media posts, and even authorized to wear and provided official department dress uniforms. That same result has happened in cities and towns all across America in the face of other tragedies too—when the light shines for a few hours or days on the incredible work done by those who serve as Dispatchers, or whatever the local variant of their job title happens to be. But the efforts and their abilities of dispatchers in FDNY and elsewhere were and are only a surprise to the uninformed and unaware. In many ways, that attention from local and national media after September 11th, 2001 failed to grasp that critical point: that the actions of the dispatchers that day were not, in fact, unique, but just one example of the capabilities they showed every day. On that day and so many others, the dispatchers went to work and did the impossible.

But how? What helps create this group of often forgotten professionals who can bring some sense of calm from the chaos? What helps explain the framework of perspectives, choices, and systems that can help a person or an organization do the impossible? The answer is, in many ways similar to our own journey through our own personal crazy days.

It starts with our own individual and internal system of either fear or doubt, denial or belief. Too often, we throw up our collective hands self-assured that a challenge or issue is just too hard to face, much less actually solve. We assume we are stuck or retreating in the ever-present shadow of our modern media world and climate of politics and culture portrayed as forever divided. But in this current era, it is more important than ever to be both bold and brave enough to see the potential and possibility in ourselves—our own ability to make even a small difference. We are not powerless. We have the potential and even obligation to persevere through distractions, doubts, noise, fear, ignorance, and the platitudes which try to pass for insight. Dime store projections of wisdom, influence, and importance can only go so far if we do not have at least a tiny amount of true self-assurance and confidence, even if we have to borrow those things from others as a starting point. Perhaps we can choose to learn, maybe for the first time, that we can do not just the simple and everyday things, but also the amazing and impossible. It begins with us—taking that first blinking step out of the bubble so carefully constructed for us by the algorithm of our own doubts and fears.

Importantly, my personal odyssey and the story of my former co-workers highlight another reality that we seem to intrinsically know but too often cast aside: we cannot do these amazing things alone. Our first steps may be solitary, but they must bring us towards others. We must strive to find or develop the support of those around us to accomplish really hard things personally or professionally. We must lean into our status as a member of community and accept that we are in this together, whether we choose to be or not. In a world where isolation is a health crisis, avatars pass as people, and the ability to anonymously hate and condemn those we have never or will never know is taken as a birthright, is it any wonder so many are in anguish. Pain so deep they are able to willingly harm others through spiritual, emotional and physical violence. One of the secrets of the group of FDNY Dispatchers I was a part of was their willingness to embrace everyone as a part of the mission when required. Sure, there were personalities and conflict. But in those hardest of shifts, everyone played their role and the collective helped to make sure everyone understood their part. There were standards, expectations, and accountability, but there was also a form of invitation and acceptance—especially if you came with the right attitude and made an effort to practice your craft. By being an effective member of the team, you were allowed to be a part of the team and that was a moment of comfort and opportunity, even in the face of extreme challenges.

It is those same crazy moments, whether personal or professional, that in the Creator's greatest ironic gift, we can find a path to reconnect with what will ultimately save us. It is obvious, or at least it should be, that if our first action is to consistently dismiss those around us as being irrelevant or unimportant, we have set ourselves and our organizations up to fail. If we assume that another person has nothing to offer or that we can do everything alone or only with people just like ourselves, our efforts on any complex task are essentially doomed. If we convince ourselves that our contributions are irrelevant or that our voice does not deserve to be heard, then we have lost before ever even starting to try.

And there-in lies a lesson from every public safety agency about the path between individual and team. If we are operating as a team, or as a community, it is important to understand the process as a two-way street. The time I spent at FDNY was not just about what my co-workers, supervisors, and trainers offered me, but what I offered them. I could have approached my willingness to be an effective team member more tactfully, but I understood and appreciated the relationship's reciprocal nature. I gave it my all and the organization gave me its best in return. They were not perfect; I certainly was not perfect. But in the best organizations perfection is recognized as such an unrealistic and ridiculous goal that it is more harmful than beneficial to even try. It is far better for the individual to focus on being even a little better today than yesterday, and better still tomorrow. Even better for the team to collectively lift up each other and remind its members that we "can" get through this—even if it's one of the most terrifying days in American History or a day of personal horror. That is made easier when we put in real effort—whether job related skills or learning to practice empathy and effective communication.

Before ever starting with the FDNY, I committed to learning as much as I could about FDNY operations, from the locations of the firehouses to the response policies for every incident to the geography of the boroughs. When I arrived, I had done my homework because that was what I knew I could do to make myself useful and set the tone for what kind of professional I wanted to be. But no matter how well intentioned, a single individual cannot force themselves into community. The people on the team must create a welcoming and safe environment for newcomers and be open and more than a little patient. Whether that is with a new neighbor from a country you have never heard of, or a new co-worker with eager ideas about essential changes in their second day on the job. New team members also must approach things from a position of understanding, even grace and patience. Although I survived being quite opinionated and having strong ideas about how things should be, that does not mean my approach was correct. There are established ways for almost every group of professionals to do things. Learning about those processes, how they work, why they are the way they are, and how they function in practice is necessary before any new person starts advocating for change. I may have made my transition easier had I invested in learning as much or more about working in teams and with people of different backgrounds than about firehouses and how many units respond to a report of a train stuck in the east river tunnel between Queens and Penn Station. Or if I had mastered the art of making coffee before starting on the job.

No better example exists of this relationship in action—of individual and team collaborating than with the emphasis FDNY fire dispatch operations placed on coffee. As a new dispatcher, it was your job to ensure that, at all times, the coffee pot in the central office was filled and coffee ready for consumption. Some shifts would drink pots and pots of coffee a day; other shifts would hardly touch it. In both cases, the least senior dispatcher on the shift was responsible for monitoring those coffee pots and keeping them filled. At the time, I did not drink coffee. As a result, I thought it grossly unfair that I be tasked with taking care of something that did not personally benefit me. I mistakenly shared that opinion with my co-workers more than a few times. It was explained to me then and in increasingly harsh language that it was not about me. It was my opportunity to take care of those on my team and demonstrate responsibility. If they could not trust me to maintain the level of the coffee pots, then how could they trust me to do other, far more critical tasks, without direction or supervision? When the busy times occurred, no one was available to follow behind and check your work. Yes, there were people to help, but each person had his or her own job in times of multiple alarm fires, hurricanes, or terror attacks. Coffee was a simple way to build the muscle memory and awareness required to take ownership of a task, ensure it was completed, and not get any reward for that effort. In other words, it was a perfect low-stress training tool that would never appear in any formal FDNY training program. This same concept applied to getting into work early and ensuring that you did shift trades for dispatchers with families who needed time off on Christmas or who were taking care of sick family members. It was never in the rule book, but it was a rule none-the-less.

Once we demonstrate an ability understand and abide by rules both written and sublime, we can begin to see ourselves as a vital part of a team and others can start to trust us as a member. Then, collectively, we can start to put into operation the processes that actually make a team effective. As the experience with the coffee pot showed, those on teams, especially those in the world of public safety, trust processes and procedures to happen a certain way every time. This permits them to avoid having to focus on the small stuff when events and incidents get crazy. They can operate from unconscious competence and avoid going to a binder of lengthy policies and procedures to figure out what to do. They can also be creative with the resources and incidents they have to manage—going beyond the basics like any good chef, artist, or writer.

This is one reason why teams can do magical things when facing stress. It is also why supervisors and managers who change too much too fast can wreck an organization with the consequences of their good intentions. And it also helps explain why our current age is so damn hard for so many people. Too much changing too fast, with lessening human support systems to help foster in the new that is coming. That is why the women and men of FDNY were able to be so effective when faced with the incredible challenge of new or even unanticipated emergencies. They had a strong foundation from which to operate.

If you knew where your units were at all times, then you knew when to pull them off of a low priority incident and re-direct them to a serious fire where they were the first arriving unit and able to rescue trapped residents in time. If you knew the operational processes at an auto extrication, you were able to discern the need to send additional units beyond the minimum to a major accident, reducing the amount of time needed to extricate people from the wreckage. Understanding the infrequent nature of reported fires in quiet areas of the borough meant the dispatcher could and would send additional units on even a single phone call reporting a fire in the wee hours of the morning—helping save not just property but lives as well. In these cases, and so many more, there was an ability to go above and beyond because we operated from a common level of understanding and knowledge—we understood our role—and our intuition led us to make great decisions as part of an effective group of committed team members fully aware of our responsibility and our mission.

Although our dispatch times (the time from taking a call for a fire to sending units) were among the best in the United States, the part of the job FDNY fire dispatch got even more right was the intangibles. They looked out for each other, supported each other, and created a world-class culture. When we look at any organization or team that does the miraculous, team members often will speak to the culture as the differentiator. In the days around September 11, 2001, and so many other events that I experienced alongside my fellow dispatchers, it was always clear that this was our differentiator. It gave us an edge and helped us make the impossible possible every single shift. Extended that understanding to our communities, our friends, and our neighbors—think for a moment how much easier it is to try new things, to venture out of our comfort zones or overcome a hardship with at least a person or two who trusts us, who we trust, and who is there no matter what.

How appropriate is it, then, that one of the legacy bell signals still used by FDNY is both a shorthand description of a serious fire or emergency and a reminder of the contributions required from each responding member? Many FDNY enthusiasts know of the radio term "10-75." This is a request for a full response of units to an incident. It sounds exciting, especially when said over the radio by the company initially arriving at a serious event—"10-75 the box 'k,' we have a fire on the second floor of a brownstone!!"

However, the more illustrative term normally happens a little while later. Generally, after the first-due chief arrives, surveys the scene, and formulates a plan of action, she or he will direct their aide to share a report on actions at the incident. In that report they will provide a significant amount of information, including the number of fire companies to be used. Not every fire company that is assigned to an incident will automatically be expected to go to work. But if the fire will require practically everyone, and maybe even additional resources, then the incident is classified as "all hands." Not some, not these, not those, but all. These two words serve as an elegant reminder of the role everyone must play when faced with the most important and serious fires or any and all horrendous challenges. It goes without saying that in my own odyssey, one that took me from a foster family, to suburbia, to the streets of New York and moments both terrifying and wonderous, I have been fortunate to have the benefit of "all-hands" many times in many different situations.

When I look back at all the events that led me to the front stoop of a Brooklyn apartment on my birthday in 2001, staring up at something beyond my understanding or imagination, I could linger on the faults, crimes, and pain represented by the screaming sirens. However, I would do so at my own peril and at the risk of disrespecting the other elements of the journey. They are the ones that hushed the sirens and the screams and made it possible to move beyond, even just to catch my breath and remind myself that I was still here, among the living, with the chance to move on to someplace just a little bit better. What element would I focus on? Thinking of my friends riding with me around Columbus's outerbelt in the aftermath of my assault, the cheering crowds of the 2002 New York City Pride Parade, or my father sharing his experiences in Vietnam helps remind me that the worst of our days do not have to be the last of our days. Finding a beacon of light to help us see our way forward does not diminish our negative experiences or make the actions of those who hurt us acceptable. Justice and atonement are important. However, as a human being or community seeking to live onward, the reminders of what makes that future life possible, even if it is just one minute in the future, are essential.

That was not just the individual lesson of my life, but also the lessons of the women and men I was honored to work with in the New York City Fire Department. They faced an insurmountable challenge with an effort that focused on what they knew how to do. They got creative, developed plans, answered phones, and tried to coordinate help for those whom the professionals knew it would be impossible to truly help, much less save. In the communications between the dispatchers and field units, even more in the phone calls between those trapped in the Towers and the fire dispatchers and 911 operators, the unimagined was found in every second of every interaction.

Many people, if not most, face heartbreaking elements of their own journeys. For some, their lives seem to be filled more with pain than anything else. I will not diminish the challenges others face or how they have pushed through. What I have learned from challenges on the individual level and those on a much larger scale is that the power of community and connection helps us through, even when there is not a happy ending with rainbows and unicorns.

Still, those connections and communities open up the possibility of the next day, a different day, and great opportunity. Sometimes, that is the only positive outcome we can hope to find. I spoke about that concept toward the end of my remarks in Westerville, Ohio in 2016. They ring just as true today.

"Today is, in many ways, a day to honor those brave and loving souls. But I would also like to challenge you to remember and share the even greater lessons of that day. We are all in this together. We all need each other.

History, especially of events like 9/11, must not be something we store in the attic, only to pull out on holidays or when distant relatives visit. History serves its best purpose when we live with it, acknowledge its lessons, and accept that it provides important insights to who and how we are today—and who and how we must be tomorrow.

"9/11 teaches us clearly something we must always remember.

"When we recognize the value and the worth of each of our fellow human beings, we can accomplish amazing things. We can solve incredible problems. We can save innumerable lives. We can bring order from chaos.

"We can help make sure that the lessons of September 11, 2001, are not…ever…forgotten."

That we have within us the ability to manage those situations and face the seemingly unimaginable was a truth whispered through almost every moment of 9/11 and its aftermath. My entire life up until 9/11 was a reminder of those possibilities, and my life since has been a refresher of that lesson.

Maybe your life, too, should you take a moment to reflect, contains a moment that seemed unbearable, but that now is just another part of your past. I hope those moments are manageable ones. That does not mean I have always been open to the lessons or that I have avoided the negative consequences. My own struggles with behaviors or mindsets that have distanced me from my hard-won insights and understandings are, in their own way, sacred reminders of the importance of our communities, tribes, and the insidious dangers of fear. Finding the light in that darkness and the power inherent in our own individual and group responses to the worst events that can befall us takes a hell of a lot of hard work. Even if it comes at intermittent moments, after years or decades of work, denial, frustration, work again, mindfulness, a cavalcade of traumas, and occasional madness, it is worth looking back and acknowledging that you were able to make it through. Celebrate the people and places that helped you gain that insight. For me, those people were friends and family along the way and the amazing group of professionals I served with as an FDNY fire alarm dispatcher. In their response to something they could not have foreseen, they modeled a possible path for us. In the process, they showed what is possible when a group of highly trained, trusted, and capable professionals has to solve a soul-destroying problem with little planning and no preparation. They showed what it meant to put all-hands to work.

This was the lesson of 9/11 for me and during my entire my time at FDNY, from coffee pots to hurricanes to that terrible, dark day in September. How I got to be a part of that organization, the twisted, crazy road that led me to the Verrazano Bridge on one Pride Sunday and marching in a Pride Parade two years later, was so much a product of milestones and miracles, some I knew about and some I did not. Through it all, the lessons continued and the opportunity to find grace and possibility, even on the darkest days, was ever present. That is the ultimate truth for anyone in public safety. No matter how tough the day is, you still have to answer the call, send help, and do your best. Just as in our personal lives, if we do not answer that call, who will? When we apply those same lessons to our personal lives and help build connections in our communities and even amongst our own personal communities then we begin to honor the events of September 11th, 2001, not as a tragedy or holiday, but as a marker that opens us to a new possibility of remembrance and action.

AFTERWORD: AT THE BORDER OF WYOMING AND MONTANA, SUMMER 2023

I did not even notice the milepost sign at first, much less the sticker. It snuck up on me, as do most coincidences when you are not expecting them. I was on my annual road trip. I try to take a solo journey each summer, ideally to someplace I have never been before. This is not just to cross places off the map where I have never been but also to open the door to ideas and possibilities that are often only accessible in the space of places and experiences unfamiliar. In the summer of 2023, my annual sojourn coincided with my goal to visit all fifty states by my fiftieth birthday. To help knock a few states off the list, I found myself standing in the late afternoon sun on the border of Montana and Wyoming. I had just made my *Close Encounters of the Third Kind*-inspired visit to Devil's Tower, a haunting formation of earth and rock in northeastern Wyoming. It was one of the few places where my expectations were significantly exceeded. It demands your attention and focus but offers no relief or explanation.

God does not provide answer keys for places like this. Surely, you can study it from a geological and historical perspective. There, of course, is a nature center and maps and guides. Sometimes, however, some places just push you down onto a bench. They force you to look at them and ponder what sort of magical, mystical, and spiritual soup created them and the people and features that populate our world. The God-made ones have that effect a little more significantly than the human-made ones, except when those places have occupied our imaginations, served as scenes in our movies, or presented themselves as physical representations of some of our most important ideals. World Trade Center Twin Towers perhaps? Our effort as humans to create inspiration and impact has always been with us; what are the pyramids, if not humankind's efforts to build the permanently inspiring? In Wyoming that day, I could not help but think about those glass and steel efforts to build a monument to who we are and what we believe. Why, in that capacity, did they serve as such tempting targets for those who wanted to cast doubt, sow fear, and call into question the American ideal? I had to wonder if they ever considered attacking the Grand Canyon, Devil's Tower, or Niagara Falls. Of course not. What does that answer say about us?

With the impact of the tower view weighing on my shoulders, I was probably primed for the next thing that happened, even if it would come as a shock. I headed for a small town in eastern Montana, where I planned to stay the night. Almost always preferring side roads and byways over interstates, I tried to navigate using my old-fashioned paper maps and my phone's mapping capability. The area's rural nature proved fatal for my cell connection and its associated data, forcing me to depend even more than I had planned on the navigation tools of my younger years. Not to worry—this was road-tripping as mother nature intended. As the sun's long rays began to lengthen further across the big western sky, turning everything below into a stew of hazy orange and shadow, I found my way to the borderline between Montana and Wyoming. It was a "eureka" moment. A giant sign proclaimed "Welcome to Montana" on one side of the road, while a sign equal in presence and stature proclaimed "Welcome to Wyoming" on the opposite side. In between them, there was a gravel pull-off and a historical marker. For those of us who are geography and history nerds, finding all this in one spot was almost too much to handle, especially since this was not planned or anticipated, but rather one of those happy "accidents" on the road.

I pulled the rental car onto the gravel and climbed out, focused on knocking off two state border signs and curious about what key bits of historical knowledge I would learn from the marker. My history geek flag flies proudly, especially on road trips. The sign was largely uninspiring. A fort had stood on this site many years before. Something about westward expansion, Native Americans, and the process of ensuring safety for the settlers as they made their way to the promised land. You can tell a lot about priorities by where the forts and the fences are and who is intended to be on each side.

I noticed in the fading sunlight just how quiet this place was. Trucks were passing by on a distant highway. They could be seen but not heard. That was the general theme of the place: lots to be seen, but a great veil of silence was enveloped in the summer heat. A bird or two sailed overhead, also seen but unheard. There were a few bugs around. Largely, this place was pure isolation and solitude. I had to wonder why the fort was needed. It seemed a waste of a canon to have it guard this prairie grass-covered land, even though I knew the occupants of that earlier place had long ago lost the battle that made the fort essential. The settlers lost, too, but in a different way. The ideal life they hoped to find at the end of whatever trail they were on just led to different kinds of trials and tribulations. There was no easy escape or easier destination. That is such a trait of ours, to this day. We try to find the better thing at the end of a road, or in a certain place, never realizing until it's too late that the most successful journeys lead us to a peace, not a place. Because of their dreams, their past was inescapable, and so was their future. That remains true for almost all of us, no matter what our journeys may be—or what events in our pasts we wish to escape.

I walked across the road to grab a photo of the signs. It was only from that different vantage point that I noticed the other sign. It was more of a post. It had originally been placed to provide mileage on the state road. Funny thing, in a way, to have a mileage post right at the border. You have only gone about twenty feet into either state, but there it is, a wooden tether to where you started, reminding you that you have not gone very far at all. Perhaps it also reminds you that there is still time to turn around.

What was added to the sign made it so much more. As often happens to signs in rural areas, it had been "decorated" by area residents and travelers. They had not been content to leave it to its original purpose. On the top of the post, someone had affixed something from far away, something that perhaps was a strange sight for many passing this spot. For me, it was a very familiar sight. It was a Maltese cross, the symbol of the fire service, and on it was a number that has become a code for all things September 11, 2001: 343. Here I was, in the middle of a place that served no real purpose, populated by competing signs announcing borders and a milepost not even worthy of a mile. In that spot, on my trip to uncover new ideas and make peace with my past, was the sticker and on the sticker, those words—the ones people think are statements, but which are actually questions: *Never Forget*.

Some people get tattoos to remind them of the events of their lives that demand to be remembered and recalled. Sometimes these are amazing successes, sometimes heartbreaking losses. I was in no need of a tattoo before, and certainly not then. All the mysterious powers decided to put something in my path to force me to remember. But the essential and eternal question remains, just as it had after my sexual assault, when I was told the story of being adopted, when conducting after-action reports of events like the Deutsche Bank Fire and Superstorm Sandy and standing in a windy memorial park over a decade after the day in my life that marked the breakpoint. Everything was one way before and everything a different way after. What do you choose to remember? What are you forced to remember? What do you have a responsibility and an obligation to remember? Once you begin to figure out the answers to those questions, then what? What do you do with that information?

Sometimes those answers are your own to answer and decide. Other times, the events of the world make the choice for you. You come to understand that the combination of experiences that put you in a certain place and time demand you speak out, call out, cry out, and share what you experienced and what you now know to be true. However, the strange and surprising reach of this is that the clarion call is for everyone to own. We have all been given lives of experience and, yes, of miracles. Each of us, if forced to review every aspect of what has led us to where and who we are, can find something to celebrate from our history and to motivate us to move forward. Hopefully, more aware of the unique gifts we bring to the word. This is true only if we own them and share them. It will not do one person any good if, in the words of scripture, it is hidden under a bushel or tossed out onto rocky ground.

Standing on the clearing, in the fleeting August Montana sun, was my answer to the question. What, exactly, should I remember? It is that I have seen and lived miracles, sometimes even in the midst of the greatest of horrors, both personal and communal. In these times of seemingly ever-increasing disconnect and fear, anger, and resentment toward others for reasons as inexplicable as they are false, perhaps some degree of leaning into the miraculous in our own stories and those of the people we encounter can be an antidote to some of what ails us. Perhaps recognizing that those miracles often happen when we value, appreciate, and welcome the stranger, can help us tear down the walls our society so enthusiastically builds. And maybe, just maybe, we can begin to live up to miraculous possibilities inherent in the best of each of us, our communities, and our world. If you looked behind the terror of the black smoke of 9/11, looked beyond the fear and the anger, and into the eyes of those who helped, consoled, carried, and sacrificed on that day, that is the sight you would see, and thankfully, it remains in view.

That was and remains my key takeaway from all the events described here. The FDNY existed long before I became a part of it and will exist long after. The story of my adoption was set in motion by a series of biological realities that my adoptive parents had to come to terms with long before I showed up on their doorstep. The circumstances of superstorms and fires, attempted assaults, and friends lost to drugs are also far out of the reach of our human desire to manage or, too often in my case, fix. But the challenge to respond as we are able, in the best way we can, is within our purview—within the span of our control. Thankfully, I have had the honor to work with teams, people, and organizations who, when given the choice, took on the challenge to be responsible. This is not just in my professional life. That same willingness to step up has characterized, in their best moments, my friends, my family, and even me on my best days. I hope it characterizes you at least sometimes as well.

In many ways, the greatest miracle of all on September 11, 2001, was that there was a September 12, 2001. That happened because of the willingness of people to step up. As New Yorkers and as members of the FDNY, we found a way forward through something unimaginable. We managed to find a balance on the narrow ledge between honoring our terrible losses and the heroic sacrifices of so many while understanding our essential role in supporting what had to continue: our own lives and the mission of our organization. We did that by recognizing the essential need for everyone to contribute, the value in each of our team members, and the fact that no person's efforts were expendable. In fact, one of the most popular slogans to come out of 9/11 was-- "All gave some, some gave all," a perfect summation of the FDNY's approach not just to major events, but its overall culture of service and contribution.

To move forward together was not optional, whether in our personal or professional lives. Doing so as part of a highly accomplished organization and a wonderful community illustrated another miracle that applies to us all: we can make it through, but only if we work together.

PHOTOS

A twenty-year old me standing beside FDNY Rescue-4 (using a reserve apparatus) while riding along with them and my friend and mentor Rich McCusker on my first ever trip to NYC in late 1994.

A "must-see" destination on one of my first visits to NYC was the firehouse of Engine Company 82 and Ladder Company 31, featured in the book "Report from Engine Company 82" by retired FDNY firefighter Dennis Smith. The neighborhood had changed significantly since the "war-years" of the 1970s, but the firehouse itself still looked much the same.

Although I was raised in Reynoldsburg, Ohio, this apartment building in downtown Columbus was where I did most of my growing up before moving to NYC. I lived in the corner apartment on the top floor.

My fire department dispatching career started here in February of 1995. The Truro Township Fire Department started in 1947 and still operates from this site, but in a newer building. The dispatch office was just inside the front door. A few years after my departure, dispatch functions were moved to a consolidated fire dispatch center in Gahanna, Ohio.

PHOTOS

A twenty-six-year-old me on the steps of my first apartment in Bay Ridge, Brooklyn, shortly after moving in—Summer of 2000.

Where my FDNY career truly began- the former Brooklyn Central Office (C.O.). The building still stands on the corner of Empire Boulevard and Washington Avenue, although the Fire Dispatchers who cover Brooklyn long ago moved to PSAC-1 (Public Safety Answering Center) in Downtown Brooklyn.

MIRACLES & MILESTONES

This is the operations floor of the Brooklyn Central Office in early 2001. Prominently featured is the map of Brooklyn Engine and Ladder Companies. Lights indicated the status of companies and helped Decision Dispatchers and Supervisors visually observe coverage and activity levels.

This is the position where my FDNY career started—Alarm Receipt Dispatcher. These positions were where most incidents started and newly hired fire alarm dispatchers had to demonstrate their skills, knowledge, attitude, and effort.

PHOTOS

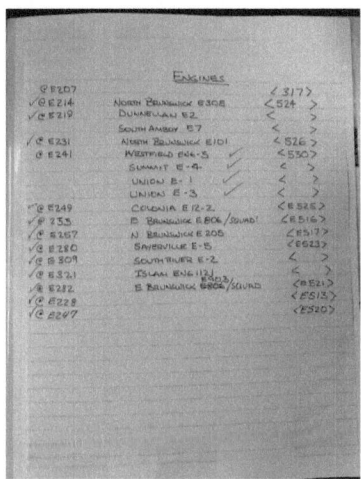

The handwritten page of mutual aid engine companies that I prepared on September 11th. I mis-heard the name "Iselin, New Jersey" and wrote "Islam" instead.

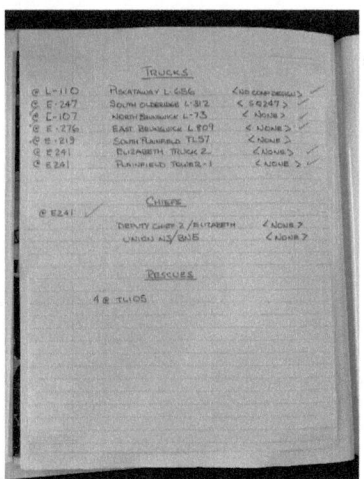

The handwritten page I prepared of locations and CAD IDs for the mutual aid ladder companies that covered empty Brooklyn firehouses on September 11th, 2001.

ACKNOWLEDGEMENTS

As with any work that attempts to capture important events that occurred over a span of time and space, an attempt to give proper credit to all those who had a role to play in shaping my experiences is probably futile at best. I will certainly leave out more than one person who deserves acknowledgment. I apologize in advance for this and thank everyone who has played a role in my career and life to date. It has been a wonderful adventure with great parts and parts that were valuable only in the lessons they contained.

I thank my parents, Jack Carver and Shirley Smalley-Carver. Dad, thankfully, is still around and living in Florida. We lost Mom in 2005, and one of my regrets is that she is not around for me to share this book with her. I also must thank my sister, Holly Carver-Gaines, her husband Matt, and my nieces Emma and Hannah for providing constant inspiration and support. I have been fortunate to have many wonderful friends, some who stayed for a season or two, some who have become permanent additions to my world. To them I say none of this would have been possible without you: Johann (and Jenn); Keith (and Erin); Doug (and Suzanne); Mory F; Eric (and Eric); Josh (and Chloe); Barb B and Bill G; Nancy M; Michael O; Ty W; Sara W; Josh D; and Chris P. A special thanks to my group of volunteer editors led by Nancy Magargal and also including Colleen Cunningham, Chris Pillar, Halene Hartman, Nicholas Vermaaten, and Joanne Kesten. And to my official editor, Donald Weise. Special thanks to

Sara W for helping make it happen in the first place. A special thanks also goes to Ann J for helping me uncover my future—what it was and what it was not. From the earliest days when I was learning about the fire service, the influence of Harry Knodel and Dan Davis and the members of the Columbus Division of Fire who let me ride along and learn firsthand about what it meant to respond to emergencies and be a part of the solution was crucial. Jim Griffiths, retired US Secret Service and Honorary FDNY Deputy Chief, also deserves special mention as an early and often supporter and champion of my dreams to live in NYC and become a part of the FDNY.

My faith has become a very important part of my life. For that, I have the congregations of Riverside Church (NYC) and The Broad Street Presbyterian Church (Columbus) to thank, along with their current and former leaders (Stephen Phelps, former Riverside Interim Senior Pastor) and Amy Miracle (Pastor) and Ann Palmerton (Associate Pastor) from Broad Street. I am also forever grateful for my amazing friends from Broad Street: Jane, Barb, Victoria, Libby, Nancy, Karen, Peggy, and all those with whom I get to spend Wednesday and Sunday Mornings and more Zoom meetings than I can count.

My other family has been the world of public safety, the fire service, 911, and my current employer, Hexagon's safety, infrastructure, and geospatial division. From those various organizations, I have to thank those who have given me critical opportunities to learn, grow, and achieve. They include Chief Jim Sharps and dispatchers Steven Rigsby and Gary Grizzle of the Truro Township Fire Department and from the FDNY: Gene Naylor; Ivan Goldberg, Deirdre Evans; Mike Fox Howard Hemsley; Edna Ceglia; Mike Esposito; Gary Greenbaum; and the many talented dispatchers, supervisors, and chief dispatchers, and the other FDNY personnel who I worked with. Serving with FDNY Dispatchers George Munch and Warren Fuchs was an honor of my professional career. To the first group I supervised in Queens, I owe both gratitude and profound apologies.

To those I instructed in the Training Unit, thank you for letting me be a part of your career and, hopefully, influence your path in positive ways. It would be impossible to name them all, but I treasured every interaction and the entirety of my experience on the floor, in the classroom, and in FDNY headquarters. I sincerely hope that my stories of your service, heroism, and dedication effectively convey the work done by generations of FDNY fire alarm dispatchers, which is still being done today.

To the person who convinced me to go to the private sector world of public safety, thank you, Ben, for seeing and suggesting a possibility I had not previously considered. From the world of Hexagon thank you to Maureen, Anna, Diane, Grant, and Chris for your encouragement and for helping keep me sane, or at least as close as I can hope to be.

Finally, none of this would have been possible without the love and support of my husband and life partner, Jayce Caleb Rentrop. A talented performer, director, and writer, he, too, believed in parts of me that I had never before seen. He provided me with both the space and constant reminders of my potential that were essential elements of completing this work. I love you more than you know, and you are by far the greatest gift that 911 ever gave me.

ABOUT THE AUTHOR

Christopher Blake Carver is a 30-year public safety veteran who has served in agencies ranging from a one seat fire/EMS dispatch office in the Truro Township Fire Department to Director of the nation's largest and busiest Fire Department Dispatch Operation—the FDNY. Along the way he has worked for some of the most significant emergency events in recent American History—from Superstorm Sandy in 2012 to the terrorist attacks of September 11, 2001.

After his time in FDNY, Christopher served as Director of PSAP Operations for the National Emergency Number Association, supporting the roll out of NG9-1-1 and the development of essential standards to improve the performance of the nation's 9-1-1 Centers. Following NENA, Christopher transitioned to the vendor side, bringing his experience and insights to Hexagon, where he serves as Director of Market Development, a cross-discipline role focusing on sales, marketing, industry engagement, and business strategy.

Outside of his full-time work, Christopher has been an Adjunct Instructor for John Jay College, an Instructor for NENA, and appears frequently on various webinars and podcasts as well as a presenter and speaker at conferences across North America and beyond.

Today, Christopher Blake Carver is also President and Executive Director of the North American Chapter of ICCRA (The International Critical Control Room Alliance) and a volunteer for Voice Corps and

Stonewall Columbus. He is also an active member of the Broad Street Presbyterian Church. He lives in the Clintonville neighborhood of Columbus, Ohio with his husband Jayce and within walking distance of a diner and at least one great neighborhood bar.

For additional information about this book, to connect with Christopher, or be the first to learn about new releases or speaking events, visit his website here: www.cbcarver.com.

TO COME

Prisoners of Lucasville (fiction)
Spring 2026

Condition Critical—the future of 911, 112, and Critical Control Rooms
Fall 2026

www.ingramcontent.com/pod-product-compliance
Lightning Source LLC
Chambersburg PA
CBHW060520080526
44586CB00012B/547